Cultures of Power in Post-Communist Russia

An Analysis of Elite Political Discourse

MICHAEL URBAN

University of California, Santa Cruz

CAMBRIDGE
UNIVERSITY PRESS

CAMBRIDGE UNIVERSITY PRESS
Cambridge, New York, Melbourne, Madrid, Cape Town, Singapore,
São Paulo, Delhi, Dubai, Tokyo

Cambridge University Press
The Edinburgh Building, Cambridge CB2 8RU, UK

Published in the United States of America by
Cambridge University Press, New York

www.cambridge.org
Information on this title: www.cambridge.org/9780521195164

First published 2010

Printed in the United Kingdom at the University Press, Cambridge

A catalogue record for this publication is available from the British Library

Library of Congress Cataloguing in Publication data

Urban, Michael E., 1947–
    Cultures of power in post-Communist Russia : an analysis of elite
    political discourse / Michael Urban.
        p.   cm.
    ISBN 978-0-521-19516-4 (Hardback)
    1. Political culture–Russia (Federation)   2. Elite (Social sciences)–Russia
(Federation)–Language.   3. Politicians–Russia (Federation)–Interviews.
4. Discourse analysis–Political aspects–Russia (Federation).   5. Russia
(Federation)–Politics and government–1991–   I. Title.
    JN6695.U885 2010
    306.20947–dc22
                                                                    2010024056
ISBN 978-0-521-19516-4 Hardback

For Veronica, one more time.

Contents

Figure and tables

Acknowledgments

The first group of people whom I would like to thank are those who sat for the interviews on which this study is based. Their names are listed in the Appendix. For me, talking with them represented the most enjoyable part of the project. Their candor and generosity of spirit amazed me not a few times, perhaps even more than their many insights into the world of Russian politics. I learned a lot from them. I also benefited from the counsel of two Russian scholars – Alexei Kuzmin and Viktor Sergeyev – whose advice during the early stages of my work proved invaluable, as did the support and encouragement of Mary McAuley and Ronald Suny.

I am particularly grateful to Vyacheslav Igrunov, a veteran of innumerable political struggles in his country and a scholar in his own right, who pulled every imaginable string to arrange the great majority of the interviews that were done. That gratitude extends, too, to Elena Alekseenkova and Vadim Sharomov who conducted some of the interviews for me while I was away from Moscow. Likewise, my thanks go to Vladimir Pribylovskii for furnishing the biographical information used in the Appendix.

The final draft of the text was informed by the encouraging and critical comments rendered by a number of scholars who had read earlier versions in whole or in part. My thanks in this regard go to: Richard Anderson, George Breslauer, Archie Brown, Craig Calhoun, G. William Domhoff, Paul Frymer, Stephen Hanson, James Hughes, Eugene Huskey, Grigori Ioffe, Cynthia Kaplan, Peter Kenez, Jonathan Larson, Ronnie Lipschutz, Aleksandr Smirnov, Vadim Volkov and Stephen White. I am likewise thankful for the opportunities to present my work in progress at Miami University of Ohio and the University of California, Berkeley. Venelin Ganev and Karen Dawisha made possible the first of these and Yuri Slezkine, the second. At later stages of the project, Paul Held, Benjamin Read and Kent Eaton fed my thinking with some very helpful suggestions on things to read. George Urban sat for many days before the computer screen painstakingly constructing a complex electronic index.

I wish to thank the Academic Senate of the University of California, Santa Cruz, for the travel grant that enabled me to make the site visit that started my research, and the National Council for Eurasian and East European Research for a generous grant that financially sustained it thereafter. Chapters 2, 4 and 5 of this volume appeared in earlier version in, respectively, *International Political Anthropology*, *Europe-Asia Studies* and *Post-Soviet Affairs*. My thanks go to the editors of those journals for permission to reprint those articles here.

Reserving pride of place for last, I make another inadequate attempt to thank my wife, Veronica, for technical and moral support, for inexhaustible patience with a person preoccupied (to his own chagrin) with thinking about the stuff of this book, and for long conversations, as well as the offhanded quip, that made that stuff better.

Note on transliteration

I have followed the standard British form for transliterating the Cyrillic alphabet into the Russian one. Hence, names such as "Yeltsin" that are regularly used in the popular press are rendered here as "El'tsin." The rare exceptions to this rule concern those Russians who have adopted a particular transliteration of their own names: thus, for instance, "Alexei" instead of "Aleksei."

I   Introduction

This book is about political subjectivities. More specifically, it concerns the ways in which political elites in Russia put together themselves and their worlds with words. It proceeds according to two basic assumptions: one, that tabulae rasae do not occur in the sphere of society, and that perception, cognition, assessment and action are fundamentally conditioned by culture; and, two, that an investigation of the political culture of Russian elites can disclose a critical dimension of their politics, identifying both what actors are able to think, say and do, and that which they cannot. Inasmuch as language constitutes the principal medium of culture, it provides a direct line of access to it. Along these lines, political culture is here conceptualized as a particular discursive formation in which individuals appear not so much as originators of their communicative acts but as relays transmitting to one another narrative messages composed and decoded on the basis of those discourses which they have internalized (Foucault, 1972; Torfing, 1999).

Below, I have more to say on the concept of discourse. For the moment, however, it may be sufficient to fix it in general terms by regarding it as a set of deep categories authorizing and governing communication in the way that, say, legal discourse would authorize that which can be said in a court of law or religious discourse, what can be uttered in a church. Consequently, the tack taken here is to investigate those cultures of power informing Russia's political class by tracing the narratives of its members back to the various discursive practices through which those cultures are expressed. Facts, in the usual sense of the term, then, are not much at issue. Nor are the particular beliefs, values or opinions expressed by political actors, although these play a contingent role in working toward an elaboration of the various discourses at play on the country's political field. By drawing on these discourses, subjects develop maps of their world enabling them to situate themselves, to locate others and to navigate their ways through the thicket of Russian politics in which reliable information is usually scarce, formal relations may not matter a whit, and things are seldom what they seem to be. Taken collectively, extant discourses – in unison or in combination – constitute the world of the subject, the subjective side of politics that is actualized in communication.

This chapter aims to accomplish a few things. One is to specify the concept of discourse as it appears in this work, a concept freighted by two difficulties. The first consists in the fact that while "discourse" has become a common term in the social sciences, its meaning has not been standardized. Some authors use it loosely, as more or less synonymous with verbal communication itself. My intention is otherwise; I wish to deploy it in a particular way, and this brings up the second difficulty: how to elucidate a usage of "discourse" – one that is not unfamiliar to many specialists in this field but one which is nonetheless counterintuitive – without side-tracking the discussion into a long exegesis of the concept itself? In the section, below, on discourse, narrative and politics, I address this issue briefly and abstractly. Accordingly, the compactness of this section – and the model of political communication that I develop in it – may appear rather dense to readers relatively unacquainted with discourse analysis. My hope is that this density will dissolve as readers progress through the body of this study where the concept is put to use and its abstract description gives way to concrete analysis.

This section of the chapter is followed by a discussion of how "discourse" is empirically interpreted in this book as narratives taken from a series of interviews with Russian political actors. This, too, is unconventional – there are not many studies employing discourse analysis on "texts" consisting of transcriptions of interview responses – and requires a little unpacking. The remainder of this chapter summarizes succeeding ones, outlining the results of the analysis as ordered by the components of my model of political discourse. Finally, in the following section, my purpose is to say a word about how the subjects in this study are constructed as participants in political discourse, a construction that draws on the notion of actors embedded in social networks and a corresponding conception of culture.

CULTURES AND NETWORKS

The present study is not the first to explore the connections between (objective) networks and (subjective) elite orientations in contemporary Russia (Buck, 2007). However, its methodology puts a different focus on the problem. On one hand, it assumes that the interior worlds of political actors do not exist *in vacuo*. Rather, their content is conditioned by context, by the webs of social relations in which actors are embedded. In order to account for this aspect of political culture, social relations among those in the political class are conceptualized as power networks, following the general orientation of those network analysts who have begun to ply their trade in countries emerging from communism (Wedel, 1998; Hughes, John and Sasse, 2002; Stark and Bruszt, 1998; Stark and Vedres, 2006; Schoenman, 2002). On the other hand, however, the standard applications of network analysis to the study of political elites do not fit the contours of my topic. They concern the positionality of actors in social space: Who is tied to whom? How are ties reticulated in network structures? The graphic representations that ordinarily accompany network analyses may offer precise depictions of social relations, yet they would be out of place in a study focusing not on those relations themselves but on the *culture* that informs them. This objective leads me to consider the concept of networks from two perspectives: as spatial-positional associations among members (power networks) that are backgrounded in the analysis; and as symbolic-communicative structures (cognitive networks) that occupy the foreground. In short, the concept of network used in this study refers to the fact that political worlds are "objectively" constituted by power networks and not by individuals per se, just as their "subjective" apprehension

and expression of politics is informed by the supra-individual phenomenon of discourse joining subjects together in cognitive networks
(White, 1992).

The notion of "cultures of power" lies at the intersection of these
two planes, referencing both the "objective" and "subjective" forms
of networks. Cultures of power express themselves as discursive
strategies, rooted in group habitus, by means of which actors on the
field of politics stake out positions yielding access to desired things – or,
to use Pierre Bourdieu's terms, to various forms of capital: symbolic,
economic and social (Bourdieu, 1986, 1991, 1998; Swartz, 2003). In the
present study, the discourses on which these strategies draw are available to analysis in the form of narratives uttered during interviews
conducted with a sample of prominent actors in Russian government
and politics. Because the objective is to trace narratives back to the
discourse(s) from which they have been drawn, I do not posit any one-
to-one correspondence between a particular actor and the discourse(s)
he or she employs in a given instance. These can change. Nonetheless,
discursive patterns do emerge from the narratives, suggesting that it is
possible to broaden the notion of network to include the medium of
discourse as a tie among individuals (Mische, 2003).

The idea that network ties can take the form of discursive
commonalities is analogous to certain concepts employed by scholars
attempting to tap the particular subjective orientations of identifiable
groups of actors in government and politics. Harold Seidman (1975),
for instance, has used the term "agency culture" for this purpose,
connoting patterns of education, professional training and sociali-
zation, and employment that instill certain habits of mind distinguishing those working in and around, say, the US Department of
Agriculture from those in the Department of the Treasury. Similarly,
Ernst Haas (1991) refers to relatively durable patterns of apprehension
and assessment found among "epistemic communities" in government and other organizations, communities forged around consensual
knowledge and belief establishing boundaries separating insiders from
outsiders. More recently, Teun van Dijk (2003) has drawn attention to

the social element in knowledge production by observing that the "common mental structures of a group" serve as a model for cognition that is manifested in the group's communicative practices.

Van Dijk's attention to this aspect of group or community – namely, communication – is the lead that I wish to follow, here. In so doing, my tack steers away from the approach of methodological individualism which takes the individual – and, in this case, his/her opinions, beliefs, ideology or whatnot – as the basic unit of analysis and, instead, attempts to view individual expression from the vantage of discursive communities from which individuals draw their identity, ascribe meaning to their practices, and interpret the world in which they act (Epstein, 2008). My objective, in brief, is to analyze the culture(s) of Russia's political class by decoding a set of interview narratives recorded with a sample of its members.

Although something called "Russian culture" is always, however implicitly, at the margins of this work, the concept of culture employed, here, differs fundamentally from the way in which it is rendered in conventional political science. Rather than a collection of beliefs and values held by individuals that are thought to cause some effect in behavior, culture appears here as meaning integral to, or coextensive with, that behavior itself, representing its internal logic or rationale (Geertz, 2000; Wedeen, 2008). It constitutes that symbolic "matrix within which that which we understand as political action takes place" (Chabal and Daloz, 2008: 21). William Sewell (1999) has introduced a distinction that helps to clarify this conception by dividing the concept of culture in two. In addition to culture, in the ordinary sense of the term's usage, as an aspect of life *abstracted* from the material realm and fit for study in its own right, Sewell argues that culture can also be regarded as a more bounded phenomenon *situated at the confluence* of meanings and practices. As an object of study, culture in this second sense problematizes the quotidian, the taken-for-granted, the common sense of the social world. It alerts the observer to the fact that this world – perhaps despite appearances – is not something ready-made but the product of human investment, an investment of meaning into the practices that comprise it. Viewed in this way, culture intersects with Bourdieu's concept of "habitus," an individual's position and way of being in the world, a disposition replete with distinctions, meanings, strategies and practices (1977, 1984, 1990, 1993, 2005). Culture, in Sewell's second sense, flows through the habitus, linking the interiors of individuals one to another by way of their background understanding of practices, creating a collective consciousness, enabling discourse.

The implications of these considerations for the present study are several. First, the object of analysis would not be construed as some objectively existing world capable of being directly apprehended by the observer, but as *representations* of the world offered by subjects within it (Geertz, 2000). Second, representations of the world are collective projects. They make sense, they are accepted as valid, within the circumference of one or another discursive community or cognitive network. For outsiders, they may appear as mistaken or even crazy. But for those sharing the same habitus informed by the same cultural practices and participating in the same discourse, they are regarded as real and, perhaps, as not even remarkable. Finally, representations of the world are structured by discourses to which individuals have access. On one hand, this implies a certain lack of ownership on the part of subjects. They instead borrow from that which is available to them, representing themselves and their world according to those discourses in which they have competence. On the other, there is no reason to suppose that subjects are confined to a single discourse, or that more than one are not present within a given habitus (Lakoff, 2008; Edelman, 1988). Individuals may be inconsistent, they may even contradict themselves, owing to the utility present in a particular discursive formulation within one context that might vanish in another.

DISCOURSE, NARRATIVE AND POLITICS

If language can be understood as society's consciousness externalized (Hodge and Kress, 1993), then discourse might be regarded as a system of categories circulating in the social world that structures and gives meaning to that very externalization (Barthes, 1968; Laclau, 2005). In so doing, discourse constrains communication. As Michel Foucault (1972: 44) has put it, "it is not easy to say something new: it is not enough for us to open our eyes ... for new objects to light up and emerge." At the same time, however, it is discourse that enables communication. It provides a set of terms, distinguished one from another by opposition, that inform any meaningful utterance (Greimas, 1983; Barthes, 1968). To take a simple example, Christian religious discourse is commonly structured by binary oppositions such as good/evil, sacred/profane, God/Satan, sin/salvation and so on. Meanings are thereby established not only in a negative sense because of the oppositions contained in each binary – "good," for instance, acquires a meaning by becoming counterpoised to "evil" – but in a positive one as well because of the ways that terms in the discourse are interlinked with one another, such that "good" would also signify "God," "the sacred" and so on (Saussure, [1972] 1983). Thus, intoning any one term immediately activates the others. In this way, the injunction to "reject Satan" simultaneously implies for the believer a whole set of prescriptions – embrace God, avoid sin, seek salvation, and so forth – just as the command "repent" would carry within itself a host of comparable associations. As such, these discursive binaries are actualized in narrative, in the spoken or written expression of individuals, which proceeds – when self-reflection is not active, which is almost always the case – unconsciously. Approached from the opposite direction, it could be said that a discourse informs the meaning of narratives generated by it (Greimas, 1990a; Grace, 1987).

Although in principle a given discourse is bounded, it should not be regarded as frozen, as some sort of doctrine. It represents the system of categories on the basis of which meaningful statements can be made, not those statements themselves. Thus, discourse is synonymous with the possibility of disputation. Within its ambit, subjects formulate and reformulate narratives as part of their discursive strategies. This aspect of communication indexes the fact that meanings are not intrinsic to particular words but to the associations that they can be arranged to convey. Spools of such associations apparent in the act of communication imply that meaningful utterances evince neither closure nor a fixed center (Torfing, 1999). The relative contingency or openness of a given discourse to usage and interpretation – not to mention the phenomenon of interdiscursivity whereby subjects employ a plurality of discourses in their narratives (Lazar and Lazar, 2004; Edelman, 1988) – is precisely what makes possible a range of communicative practices, among them, politics (Howarth and Stavrakakis, 2000).

Political discourse can be regarded as a creative synthesis of elements belonging to other forms of discourse that are not in themselves political. These elements are set out schematically in Figure 1.1. In order to show how they enter into political discourse, how they become constitutive parts of it, I need a concept of politics that can bind them together in the same way that a quantum of energy might bind together atoms in a molecule. For that purpose I enlist Max Weber's meditation on politics set out in his renowned essay, "Politics as a Vocation" ([1919] 1946). Thereafter, I qualify and extend his conception by linking it to the discourse theory of Jürgen Habermas. This enables me to develop an ideal type for the concept of political discourse based syntactically on the rudiments of language's organization of the world: namely, the relations among subject, object, indirect object and verb (action).[1] By building on these syntactic categories, I aim to ground the model in the irreducible elements of language itself, while simultaneously providing it with a maximum degree of generality for its application. Here, I follow the approach developed by Yurii Lotman for whom language, as a set of symbolic relations and rules for their transformation, functions as

---

[1] The syntactic aspect of this ideal type follows A. J. Greimas's (1983) actantial model of narrative. The elements in it constitute discourses in their own right as well as elements in a larger discourse of politics. In referring to them separately, I call each a discourse; when viewing them in this second way as components of a larger construct, I call them "elements" or "dimensions" of political discourse.

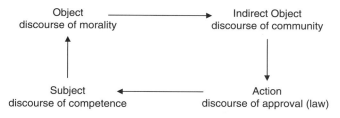

Object
discourse of morality

Indirect Object
discourse of community

Subject
discourse of competence

Action
discourse of approval (law)

FIGURE I.I The elements of political discourse.

the primary modeling system for all forms of culture – art, religion, politics and so on (Zylko, 2001).

On the basis of the four syntactic categories, the model overlays semantic ones: namely, four distinct discourses that are interwoven in political narratives. In correspondence with syntax's "subject," "object" and so forth, these discourses are, respectively, discourses of competence, morality, community and approval (law).[2] Here, discourse concerns the ability, and the way in which, to talk about the subject, object and so on. It does not stand for those things themselves. At this level of abstraction, my argument is that political discourse is instantiated by the identification of some object represented as a good to be secured by a subject (claiming the competence to do so) on behalf of a community constituted by law and approving (or not) the subject's actions through the medium of legal discourse. A certain homology therefore prevails between the elements of syntax and the four discourses represented in the model. In the same way that syntactic rules must be followed in order to make sense, so political discourse is stunted without incorporation of all four of its elements. When full incorporation is not the case, as is generally true of the narratives recorded in this study, distortion occurs (Habermas, 1970).

To illustrate, take the syntactically incomplete phrase "He him." In this instance, communication is distorted inasmuch as the receiver of this message is unable to decode it. There is no verb and it

---

[2] The substantive side of the ideal type draws on the work of Murray Edelman (1977, 1988).

is unclear whether "him" refers to a direct or to an indirect object. Similarly, with respect to political discourse, comparable incompleteness produces its own distortion. Messages that systematically exclude either who the subject is, the good that he or she pursues, the beneficiary of his/her action or its justification cannot offer their recipient the information required to participate in political discussion. Can, for instance, the purported good, say, public safety, be accepted without consideration of its justification? Would provision of this good include torture? Warrantless detention? Mass surveillance? Similarly, who is the subject securing this good, state officials or vigilante groups? When reference to one or more of these elements of political speech goes missing, messages are garbled.

In the present study, the preponderance of distortion is traced to the negligible role in Russian political discourse performed by the two elements referring to a public – community and approval – along with a concomitant over-reliance on the elements associated with the personal: competence and morality. Speakers show an almost uniform disregard for law, even as some of them lament its absence. Likewise, their statements sometimes include reference to community but, with rare exception, not to a community comprised of legally constituted citizens whose approval or disapproval might represent a standard for conduct. In the following chapter, I show that this imbalance in the discursive structure is consistent with patterns of social relations prevailing in Russia.

At this point, two general observations are in order. First, by conceptualizing political discourse as an ideal type, the model gestures toward the universal: political discourse in any place or time can be analyzed according to its categories. Cautions, rightly, go up in this respect, because of the possibilities of an ethnocentric identification of the ideal type with some actually existing polity that appears to resemble the ideal, against which others, which do not, would appear as deficient or perverse (Chabal and Daloz, 2006). However, this concern neither invalidates the use of an abstract universal to investigate and characterize a concrete particular, nor would it rule out the chance that projects inspired by abstract universals can enter the realm of practice (Bourdieu, 1998). Second, the elements in the model do not represent discursive practices unrelated to one another. Rather, they are connected dialectically in the sense that they interpenetrate each other in mutually constitutive ways. For instance, claims to competence do not exist independently of moral considerations concerning how this competence is to be exercised and whom it is to serve, just as notions of the good do not stand apart from the pragmatic question of who might be capable of securing it. Moreover, as this study shows, the eclipse of some elements (here, law and community) has consequences for the ways in which the others function.

The model's application to actual political narratives by no means rules out interest-based strategic communication, the quest for power for its own sake, greed, chicanery, lying and other practices common to the world of actual politics. Rather, it simply asserts that these things will not appear openly in political narratives. The price exacted for engaging in political speech is to verbally conceal or transform them by means of the categories in the model. The cases of strategic communication in bargaining and compromise, which are also not direct manifestations of the ideal type, likewise refer back to it, framing the object as "the best that can be achieved under present circumstances" or identifying certain sectors of the community as deserving of particular consideration. To recapitulate, political discourse concerns itself with some good to be achieved by those said to be capable of securing it on behalf of a designated community (public) that is able to register its approval, to dispute or reject that action via a discourse of legality.

The epoxy holding these four elements in place under the sign of political discourse is provided by Weber's concept of politics. For him, political discourse would be state-centered inasmuch as it expresses, however obliquely, an interest in power. Power, in turn, must be pursued in order to accomplish some public purpose, but this purpose must itself be tethered to an ethic of responsibility whereby the politician abstracts himself from the political fray in order "to let realities work upon him with inner concentration and calmness. Hence his distance to things and men" (Weber, 1946: 115). In so doing, the politician is required to privilege his sense of real, over desired, outcomes, taking a principled responsibility for the actual consequences of his actions and thus avoiding the Scylla of "exploiting 'ethics' as a means of being 'in the right,'" while simultaneously escaping the Charybdis of vanity induced by the seductions of power which quashes his sense of social purpose (Weber, 1946: 116–118).

Weber cautions that although these aspects of the political might be brought into an imperfect harmony, they individually tend to subvert the enterprise of politics. Just as "it is in the nature of officials with high moral standing to be poor politicians," so morality's absence represents "self-intoxication" for the politician, a "sin against the lofty spirit of his vocation" (1946: 95, 116). Politics thus represents a paradox wherein ethics are required but do not admit to any universal formulation, wherein truth is mandated but not in any absolute form. Correspondingly, the language of politics is a contingent one that advances strategic interaction by displaying a receptivity to difference and conflict while rationalizing their manifestations in ways making it possible to live with these very things (Green, 1987). Political discourse therefore includes elements that are both constitutive and subversive to its enterprise, a tension required to reach decisions taken on an undecidable terrain (Torfing, 1999).

The interplay of power and morality informing this conception reflects Weber's fundamental categories structuring action: *Zweckrationalität*, an instrumental rationality referring to the act of "making use of ... expectations (concerning the behavior of others or that of physical objects) as 'conditions' or 'means' for the successful attainment of the actor's own rationally chosen ends"; and *Wertrationalität*, or value-rationality, which concerns ends selected by reason and valued for their own sake (Weber, 1947: 115). However, whereas Weber draws an ironclad distinction between these two forms of rationality and focuses on *Zweckrationalität* – for which "absolute values are always irrational" (1947: 117) – as the vector pointed toward modernity, Habermas has repeatedly sought to overcome that division by including *Wertrationalität* as an inescapable dimension of the modernizing process, a potential opened in communicative inter-action that gestures toward the possibility of organizing life on the basis of rationally chosen norms (Habermas, 1971, 1974, 1975, 1979, 1984, 1987, 1998). Indeed, he has explicitly criticized Weber on this score, chiding him for acknowledging both forms of reason and then foreclosing the prospect of using value-rationality as a second criterion for charting the development of state and society according to a prac-tical rationality anchored in the consideration of ends as well as means (Habermas, 1984).

Habermas has theorized the conjunction of these two forms of rationality under the category "legitimation." On one hand, he acknowledges that legitimation is expressed – as the word would indicate – as a relationship prescribed by positive law. But, on the other, he recognizes that positive law alone is inadequate to the task of legitimation because – functioning both as a steering mechanism of the state and as an expression of society's moral code for regulating itself – law's status can be ambiguous and at times contradictory (Habermas, 1987). The supplement, so to speak, is provided by the normative order itself that is in part captured in legal acts and, in part, stands outside of them as a basis for critique. Thus, legitimacy implies both the procedural rationality represented by law and the notion of "rightness" stemming from society's normative order that is itself open to argument and, therefore, to rationalization (Habermas, 1975, 1979, 1984, 1987).

This confluence of law and morality expressed in the concept "legitimation," however, should not disguise the fact that the nor-mative systems to which they refer are structured in fundamentally different ways. Legal right is no mere copy of moral right. Whereas morality appears as a relatively durable symbolic system rooted in cultural knowledge, law is a more adaptable mechanism, capable of responding to change by enlisting the compulsion of the state

(Hart, 1994). Moreover, while morality is "restricted to a narrow range of action," its coupling with the legal system allows it to be "spread to *all* spheres of action" (Habermas, 1998: 188, emphasis in original). In so doing, law represents a more rationalized normative order, "*leaving open* the motives for conforming to norms [while enabling] citizens to *reach an understanding* about the rules of their living together [thus] stabilizing behavorial expectations" (Habermas, 1998: 83–84, emphasis in original). When the complexities attending modern life overburden the moral calculus, law stands in reserve as a set of norms mediating social relations.

However, it should be emphasized that positive law is not equivalent to legal discourse which, in the conception of political discourse set out here, is the means by which a community registers its approval of state action. To claim that law involves a discourse of approval is to say neither that a certain law has approved something nor that a given law has itself been approved by the community. Both of those instances would refer to a result, whereas the concept of legal discourse refers to a process occurring in communicative space in which voices of approval and disapproval contend about the means, conditions and procedures for approving something, as well as about that something itself. As I wish to show, below, law in this broader sense of process represents a practice conditioned by the integrity of the community in question, an integrity mediated by law and its attendant discourse.

In Russia, law has traditionally played a very weak role in regulating social behavior. To be sure, law's relative import has varied over time, occasionally increasing in salience (at least, discursively) only to recede again (Berman, 1961; MacFarlane, 2003). Nonetheless, the modal pattern suggests that law as a force capable of constraining the conduct of actors in politics and society – especially top officials in the executive apparatus of the state or powerful figures associated with them – tends toward nil. That generalization would appear to hold across the field of legal institutions including the courts (Solomon, 1987, 2007, 2008; Volkov, 2004; Huskey, 2002), the legislature

(Huskey, 1990, 2007; Foster, 1993), and the executive (Gel'man, Ryzhenkov and Brie, 2003; Gel'man, 2004; Volkov, 2002). Within the context of Russian cultural practices, law resembles more the injunctions of those who happen to occupy state offices than it does an impersonal – much less rationally formulated – instrument for regulating social relations. As such, as Marina Kurkchiyan has observed, law enjoys almost no place in the country's sense of the real. It does not merge with the actual course of one's calculations and goal-directed actions but appears as an artificial requirement set in place by an alien authority – something to be paid lip-service, something to be negotiated, eluded, subverted or cheated, but not something to be followed for its own sake (Kurkchiyan, 2003).[3]

As shown, below, the interview results recorded in this study amply attest to these observations and suggest reasons for them – above all, the personalization of authority relations tied to the importance of power networks within the state. Therefore, the discourse of law does little to *"offset the weaknesses of a morality that exists primarily as knowledge"* of the moral code itself (Habermas, 1998: 114). As a consequence, those in complex societies such as Russia that lack the reinforcement of a normative order expressed in legal relations are likely to experience a palpable deficit of morality in social interaction. Without law on which to rely, attention falls on moral criteria as the sole means for regulating social relations, a practice yielding an unending demand for morality that keeps close company with the knowledge of its absence in practical matters.

Just as the weakness of law is experienced as an absence of morality, so both of those shortcomings in Russia can be traced to a deeper problem of community. As a designator of membership in a legally constituted community, law confers rights and obligations on community members. It creates an inclusive "we," a community of

---

[3] Yuri Lotman (1990) has argued that historically Russian culture has been inhospitable to notions of law and contract, taking them to be Satanic. Thus, within this code, cheating – as represented by the figure of the trickster in folklore – is marked positively.

citizens – *of equals* – based on mutual recognition. Historically – whether in the estates of the *ancien régime* or the politically based distinctions among status groups introduced under communism (Jowitt, 1992) – community in Russia has been fractured. As illustrated in the following chapter, the absence of legal equality tends to channel collective action away from the public sphere and toward personalized, informal practices. In a given instance, these practices generate, sustain and are, in turn, predicated upon an exclusive "we" expressed in social consciousness as fragmented community whose subjects draw thick lines between "our own" and "others" (Ries, 1997; Pesmen, 2000; Shevchenko, 2008). Membership in these categories can easily shift even while the practice of employing them goes on undisturbed.

In the same way that law constitutes modern community, it is precisely standing in a community that allows each of its members "to be taken account of or listened to" and thus to take part in law's discourse of approval (Foot, 1977: 237). Statutory law represents the outcome of this process whereby communities register their approval. To illustrate: polygamy in Western countries may elicit the community's moral censure but, inasmuch as the polygamist is likely acting according to another moral code, this would matter very little. Community approval (or, here, disapproval) would be actualized in legal discourse and, ultimately, in legislation and subsequent enforcement.

The eclipse of a discourse of approval issuing from the fracture of community impedes the formation of a collective phenomenon, "the people," as a category in social consciousness relevant to law and politics. The principal role of this category in politics lies in the construction of what Habermas calls "communicative power," the signification that the people approve or disapprove of something. As he puts it, the discursive construct, "the people," constitutes those

> "subjectless" forms of communication circulating through forums and legislative bodies ... Political power is differentiated into communicative power and administrative power ... Only in this anonymous ["selfless"] form can ... communicatively fluid power

bind the administrative power of the state apparatus to the will
of the citizens. [Communicative power] only takes effect in the
circulation of reasonably structured deliberations and decisions.

(Habermas, 1998: 136)

Russia's fractured sense of community seems unable to sustain
this "subjectless" variety of communication as an actual form of
power bearing on government and politics. Rather, among those in
the interview sample, community appears in two versions, each
internally contradictory. One version exists on a personal level. Here,
respondents' narratives portray interpersonal relations among those
in their respective power networks as thick, warm, intimate and
suffused with moral responsibilities to one another. Their characterizations of other political groupings are correspondingly negative,
laced with invective about their immorality, incompetence or both.
The second version of community pertains to the national level. In
this respect, their characterizations are bifurcated into positive –
although rarely expressed – articulations of the Russian people in
the abstract and, on the other hand, concrete representations of the
Russian people that almost invariably depict them as politically
ignorant, gullible, inert, and in need of (their) help.

The issue of help, of course, involves the *desideratum* of
competence. If there is a good to be pursued on behalf of some community, then the discourse of competence represents that communicative
space conducive to addressing the question of who can best secure it.
For Russia's political class, the interviews recorded here provide a
single answer: "professionals." But that term is interpreted in dichot-
omous fashion: one group – those who have entered into political
activity after having pursued professional careers in other fields –
insist that their specialized knowledge and professional ethics have
equipped them with the requisite competence; those in the other
group, professional politicians, argue that their experience supplies
the essential know-how to achieve real results. In both instances,
however, their narratives are heavily shaded with moral claims,

constructing themselves discursively as those who act for the community out of some inner sense of duty and who are concerned little, if at all, about the community's actual approval of their action. This pattern seems consonant with both the community's weak representation in social consciousness as a public and with the double-duty imposed on moral discourse in compensation for the weakness of law.

That overburdening of moral categories coinciding with the weak role of law in Russian politics not only helps to account for the rather heated moral claims made by many in the political class. It also reflects the distance separating political actors from society because weak law is incapable of sustaining a discourse of community approval. To be sure, interview subjects make positive mention of such things as laws and constitutions, but these are framed as benefactions performed by those in the political class for the sake of society. Their narratives never convey any systematic or sustained appreciation for law as either the expression of popular will or as a social regulator, as the medium in which conflicts can admit to both resolution and ongoing dispute, as the source of legitimation. This absence, then, is a significant "presence" in Russian politics, conditioning the overall, and incomplete, synthesis of political discourse. The Russian political animal, as it were, appears to walk on only three legs.

METHOD AND SAMPLE

The present study applies discourse analysis to a corpus of thirty-four texts generated by that same number of interviews – each lasting between 45 minutes and roughly two hours – conducted between May 2005 and June 2006.[4] The interview subjects were drawn from prominent members of Russia's political class: government ministers (including prime and deputy prime ministers), leaders of political

---

[4] I conducted twenty-four of the interviews myself. The remaining ten were carried out by Elena Alekseenkova, a graduate student in political science at the Russian State Humanities University (eight), and Vadim Sharomov, a journalist in Moscow (two).

parties, deputies of the State Duma, officials in the Administration of the President and others (see Appendix). In order to preserve anonymity, they are identified here by a code referencing their membership in five broadly defined groups: the administration of Mikhail Gorbachev (all of whom are labeled A, plus a number identifying each individual); the first (1991–1993) and second (1993–1997) El'tsin administrations (members labeled, respectively, B and C, each with an identifying number); the democratic opposition (members of the political party Yabloko, labeled D plus a reference number) and individuals identified with the administration of Vladimir Putin (labeled E plus a reference number). Inasmuch as a given individual may have been associated with more than one group – for instance, someone who held high office in both of the El'tsin administrations, or someone active in politics during the Gorbachev years who later joined the Putin-era cohort – the five categories are somewhat blurred. These categories represent cohorts and not necessarily discursive or cognitive networks. Nonetheless, the results here show that the cohorts in large measure do correspond to groups of people sharing more or less distinct narrative programs, thus indicating that cognitive networks are identifiable in the sample.

The five cohorts under consideration not only were active under differing political circumstances – late-communism, revolution, reform and Putin's version of restoration – but their specific experiences in government and politics tend to reflect their career backgrounds and, thus, the capital that they brought with them to their jobs. Temporally, Marc Garcelon's (2005) notion of the 1990s as an "interregnum" in Russian politics is useful for sorting out these differences in the sample. It would refer directly to those in the first and second El'tsin administrations who entered politics with cultural capital accumulated during their earlier academic careers, riding to power on the crest of the democratic movement that they, in turn, eviscerated by pursuing economic policies impoverishing the vast majority of individuals and political solutions, such as canceling and rigging elections, that consigned the citizenry to the sidelines.

"Interregnum" would also refer indirectly to the democratic opposition who also emerged from intelligentsia backgrounds but who distinguished themselves sharply from their counterparts in El'tsin's governments by resigning and/or refusing appointments in the executive, and by assuming a very critical, if not altogether hostile, posture toward many of those in the El'tsin administrations. Finally, "interregnum" severs the putative continuity between the Gorbachev and El'tsin reforms and instead establishes a connection between the Gorbachev and Putin-era cohorts. As the narratives recorded for this study demonstrate, the last two groups share a version of political discourse that is far more sensitive to the exigencies and subtleties of governing, a reflection of the practical political-governmental work that characterizes their career histories and the accumulation of social capital attending that enterprise.

These differences and similarities in respondents' narratives therefore connect individuals both within and across groups in the sample. To illustrate, members of the first and second El'tsin administrations speak about competence and morality in ways that distinguish them sharply from the Gorbachev-era and, especially, the Putin-era cohorts. For the El'tsin groups, competence tends to be represented as specialized knowledge, while morality refers both to the social good that they claim to have pursued and to the ways in which they went about pursuing it. In certain cases, their narratives might falter in accounting for failures in competence, and for political outcomes that do not measure well on the scale of moral values. In such instances they sometimes introduce hyper-semiotic constructs – "We saved the country from famine" and "We prevented a global nuclear holocaust" – that shift discursive gear from practical considerations to eschatological ones. But, in so doing, they abandon neither their basic concepts of competence and morality nor their claims to them. The narratives of those in the Gorbachev- and Putin-era cohorts, on the other hand, reflect a very different version of competence, one that involves political know-how rather than specialized knowledge. Likewise, their version of morality is more situational and, in the case of the Putin group, does not explicitly address any larger social purpose. In contrast, the Yabloko contingent speaks the language of the El'tsin-era cohorts – specialized knowledge and principled morality – even while they sharply differ with El'tsin's people on what these things have meant in practice.

With respect to the questions posed to these respondents, I have departed from the conventions often informing survey work in the social sciences. Because my purpose has been to generate texts that might be analyzed for their discursive content at a deep or fundamental level, there is no pre-set scheme of interpretation here that is built into the questions themselves. Were I concerned with, say, the traits of individuals, things would have been different. The questions in that case would seek to elicit specific replies relevant to some analytic category such as "trust," "tolerance" or "ideology." In the present instance, however, the objective has been to get interview subjects to talk at some length about their experiences in, and apprehension of, the world of politics. Thus, in consultation with two Russian political scientists – Victor Sergeyev and Alexei Kuzmin – I formulated open-ended queries associated with broad themes that the interview subjects could interpret as they chose to do. And often, they interpreted them in markedly different ways. Although this would represent a serious problem were individuals the focus of the study – namely, responses could not be measured because respondents were in fact not addressing the same questions – it facilitates an alternative research strategy concerned with the supra-individual phenomenon of discourse. Subjects' interpretations of the open-ended questions, in this instance, represent an essential element of investigation because they signal the particular discourse(s) employed by the subjects in formulating their responses.

The questions put to interviewees were the following:

- What are/were the most significant moments in your political career? At which times did it seem to you that you exercised the greatest influence on political events in the country? What helped you realize your objectives? What hindered?

- What lessons could be drawn from your experience? How would you formulate principles for the successful realization of political goals in Russia?
- Which personal qualities help to achieve one's goals in politics? In what measure are these qualities connected with the ability to establish good personal relations with other people?
- From your point of view, what is the role of moral principles in politics? Can you confirm your point of view with examples, not necessarily drawn from your own experience?
- What was your relation to the following events and how do you relate now to the actions of the primary participants in them? August 1991. The Belovezh Accords. The events of autumn, 1999.

Because the central objective of each interview has been to encourage the respondent to speak as candidly as possible about his/her experience and subjective orientation to it, I have adopted the method of the "active interview," according to which information is produced by the collaborative efforts of both the interviewer and the interviewee (Holstein and Gubrium, 2004). For his/her part, the interviewer would be required not only to explain thoroughly his/her purposes to the interviewee, but to share with the respondent his/her own thoughts on the interview topic. This approach is intended to reduce the distance between interviewer and respondent and thus to stimulate a dialogue that has greater potential to unearth important information, qualifications and assessments than do monologic responses to set questions. Specifically, my intention has been to generate "collective stories" from the respondents, descriptions of the world and their places in it that diverge from authorized accounts of reality (Miller and Glassner, 2004). The generation of these stories is triggered by the interviewer's prompt, contained in the first question, and sustained by follow-up questions which probe the respondent about the significance that events, persons, institutions and so on have held for him or her.

Two objections might be made to this method: selection and size. Regarding the former, why were these respondents – all of whom can be identified broadly as belonging to the "liberal" wing of Russia's political class – chosen, and not communists or nationalists? The answer in part would depend on discourse, on the fact that Russia's anti-communist revolution has authorized the introduction of a capitalist order and thus marginalized communist discourse to the point that the largest nominally communist organization in the country – the Communist Party of the Russian Federation – has itself abandoned it (Urban, 1998). Elements of a nationalist discourse, however, do inform the narratives of some respondents, particularly those from the Putin-era cohort, but not only them, recording nationalism's influence even while nationalists themselves have remained on the sidelines. Thus, the selection of these interviewees speaks to the issue of including in the sample representatives of Russia's political class who have been involved with the dominant tendency in the country since *perestroika*, the institution of a capitalist state.

A second issue associated with selection bears on the matter of representativeness in another sense: randomness. Does a collection of interviews conducted with this fraction of Russia's political class represent the discursive circumference of the entire class itself? There is no way to be sure about this. Heavy constraints on selection prohibited building any thought of randomness into the process of tapping people for interviews. Especially with respect to those occupying official positions when the fieldwork was conducted, access was extremely difficult to secure, and not a few potential subjects declined to be interviewed. Rather like the personalized networks discussed in the following chapter, selection proceeded through intermediaries acting on my behalf who contacted acquaintances in the political class and offered assurances that I had no political purpose in gathering information and that it would be used in a purely scholarly work.

Then, there is the issue of sample size. Bracketing the matter of random selection, does the number of interviews recorded constitute a representative sample? The standard view in the empirical social sciences would respond to this question of sample size by raising issues such as degrees of probability, levels of statistical confidence and the like. It seems to me that this line of thinking is not relevant in the present context. It tacitly presupposes a model of perception according to which there is some world, existing unto itself, which the analyst is able to represent in a manner not fundamentally different from the act of taking up pen and paper in order to represent, say, a building, a tree, or a lovely face. For actors in the social world, the same logic would prevail – they are believed to have opinions or traits or beliefs, and it is the analyst's job to capture and to analyze them. Having collected some number of these things as a sample, the issue then becomes a matter of the statistical probabilities governing inferences from them to a larger population. Because the present study concerns a very different order of things, that perceptual program seems inappropriate. I am interested in something that does not belong to individuals themselves, namely, discourse. I therefore want to examine the ways in which they appropriate and use it – processes that do not presuppose an identification of a subject with a particular discourse – in order to determine the actual discourses at play on the political field. Consequently, the orientation here is not to expect reality (one's opinions, values and so forth) to be represented in speech but to regard speech itself as constituting reality, and thus the object of investigation in its own right. The point would be to locate within speech that cognitive program making it possible. From this vantage, sample size is by no means irrelevant – one needs a plurality of subjects in order to trace out the ways in which discourse is deployed in given instances and to make corresponding comparisons – but it is not determinant.

Finally, the substantive chapters of this book contain a goodly number of authorial interventions, as I attempt to interpret and to categorize the remarks of those interviewed. However, in many instances I have found such interventions to be superfluous. It seems that often the words of the subjects are themselves sufficient to indicate the codes from which they have been drawn.

OUTLINE OF THE BOOK

The argument in this book proceeds on the assumption that social relations and the consciousness of actors form a unity (Marx and Engels, [1932] 1965: Lukacs, [1919] 1971). This conception posits no causal link between the two. Whether social relations cause people to think in certain ways or their ways of thinking produce certain social relations are not its concern. Instead, the focus is on how each of these aspects of the world represent the condition for the other. To begin on the side of social relations, this conception would hold that they include in themselves a number of background practices, tacit understandings among participants of their habitus, which enable them to decode speech, actions and institutions (Bourdieu, 1977, 1984, 2005). Without these understandings, the world would be misconstrued or unintelligible (Goffman, 1981; Kharkhordin, 2000). For example, were I ignorant of background practices in a Russian sauna, on visiting one I might think that I had entered a torture chamber: here are nude men in an uncomfortably warm room, some whipping others with birch rods. Then, when I noticed that the rods were exchanged so that their previous holders could now themselves be whipped, I might imagine that I was present at the meeting of some sadomasochist club. The meaning of these practices would become clear only when I learned that they had to do with something else – health, that which in this instance unites practices and the relations among the parties with their consciousness of those practices and relations.

Because I am interested in the consciousness of Russia's political class as manifest in its discourse, the following chapter takes up the matter of social relations in which discourse is embedded. In it I develop a model of social relations in post-communist Russia which contrasts sharply with the conventional concepts of civil society employed by most Western observers. This model – "Civil Society II" – is predicated on the understanding that *embodied* forms of capital (those that are inseparable from the persons who possess them) of the social and cultural varieties are of much more consequence in Russian politics and society than is *disembodied* economic capital (which is detached from its owner in the form of money or that which can be converted to it) that predominates in the West. As a result, social relations in Russia are both thicker (appearing as strong ties among actors) and more diffuse (relevant to a broader array of needs-satisfying endeavors) than the conventional model of civil society would allow. The principle of political organization reflects this pattern of social relations as well. Instead of voluntary associations that the civil-society model posits – based on the formal equality of subjects that reflects the dominant role of disembodied (economic) capital in ordering social relations – in the Russian instance that role is awarded to "power networks," based not on putative equality but on personalized (unequal) relations that animate the formal institutions of state, economy and society.

I then employ the interview narratives to explore the validity of the model. I find that its categories – especially that of "power networks" – are consonant with the stories told by respondents. I infer from this coincidence a fit between the model and the phenomenal worlds of the interview subjects, and interpret that fit to indicate a unity prevailing between social relations and a consciousness of them. Again, this is not a causal inference. Rather, the point is that the social relations indexed by the model are intelligible to actors because of their knowledge of the background practices that they include. That knowledge engenders the consciousness required for actors to participate in, and thus reproduce, those same relations. Along these lines, the actors' discussion of social relations introduces a difference between "clans" and "teams" as varieties of power networks. The former span the border separating state from society and display a diffusion of purpose. Respondents reserve the term "clans" for others, assigning to it pejorative adjectives such as "mafia." "Teams," however, is almost invariably used by respondents to reference their own network. Yet it is also possible to introduce an analytic distinction here, which construes "teams" as intense group interaction oriented to a more limited domain of activity. In the case of teams, a familial discourse of community prevails as a template for conceptualizing interpersonal relations that is highly gendered, assigning roles and responsibilities to "papa," "mama" and "sons/brothers." This discursive formulation inhibits the formation of community at macro-level, even while it solidifies and deepens it with respect to face-to-face interaction.

The following three chapters are organized according to the elements in the political-discourse model (Fig. 1). Chapter 3 addresses the discourse of community. It investigates the ontology posited in community's discursive construction, the view among respondents that there are social phenomena that exist unto themselves, apart from any human agency. Obviously, this view is illusory when it comes to the social, and it can itself be explained by the influence of culture on habitus. The respondents' narratives on social being are divided into two broad categories – state and society – each representing an aspect of community.

The interview narratives evince a dual consciousness with respect to the state. On one hand, it appears as a thing impeding their efforts and derailing their purpose. This visage of the state perceives it as a brick wall of bureaucracy. On the other – and at more proximate range – respondents tell stories in which the bricks seem to have lives of their own. These narratives are congruent with the notion of power networks functioning within the executive and record the negligible role that law plays in the country's political discourse, appearing in this instance as a deficit of legality that fails to contain executive power and its private appropriation.

The topic of society also appears in thing-like guise. Contrary to discourses of the modern state in which "the people" comprises the central category, respondents' narratives tend to denigrate, rather than to celebrate, this construct. The discourse of community, by implication, is thus weakly represented in the interview sample. There are two exceptions: one respondent spoke of popular political involvement during the late *perestroika* period; and another recounted how ongoing casework on her part inspired considerable citizen involvement in her election campaigns. All others addressed the topic of the people using herd-like terms, portraying the population as politically inert, uncomprehending, in need (but unappreciative) of their benefactions, vulgar and degraded, and easy to manipulate. Thus, in correspondence with a relative absence of law, the language of Russia's political class is little informed by a notion of national community. The idea of belonging seems mainly confined to one's own network, rather than to some larger collectivity. This leaves the categories of morality and competence to do the heavy semiotic lifting.

Chapter 4 is organized around the topic of morality. It begins with a word on two dimensions of political discourse relevant to securing a recognizable good for the community – law and morality – and notes how the former is neither a valorized component of Russian culture nor an issue that, with a few exceptions, respondents have addressed. As if to compensate for law's absence, the interview subjects stressed the importance of morality, even while lamenting the fact that political practice collides with moral precepts. In the extreme instance, twelve members of the sample – including government ministers, a leader of a political party, members of the national legislature and directors of policy-making organs in the executive – denied that they had actually had political careers; such, it seems, is the degree of opprobrium associated with politics. The robust, if not excessive, discussion of morality by interview subjects corresponds to their perceptions that there is little if any of it to be found in political practice.

The narratives in this chapter span a range bordered at one end by an expressed commitment to a version of morality permitting no compromise with moral principles and by another version interpreting morality as loyalty to one's group. Obviously, one version shares nothing in common with the other. Those consistently embracing the principled variant, not surprisingly, have spent their political careers at the greatest remove from state power. For them, abstract morals represent both a claim to self-worth and a position from which to criticize power holders. Conversely, those sponsoring the conception of morality as loyalty occupied political office at the time at which the interviews were conducted. This second group prized "results" over principles and argued that results depend on ignoring, evading or bending moral strictures. Hence, morality in political life is reduced by some of them to not lying, by others to exercising some level of deception for the sake of results and by one to sheer group loyalty, pure and simple. For this group, a particular version of morality appears consonant with their practices and with the social relations in which those practices are embedded. Those in the other cohorts, using the trope employed for the other as noted in Chapter 2, referred to this pattern as "clan morality," the morally sanctioned amorality evinced by individuals conducting the affairs of their respective power networks.

The salience of the moral dimension in Russian political discourse not only serves to compensate for the perceived absence of law in the country's political practice, but its prolix expression in the interview narratives also underscores the equally perceived absence of morality in politics as well. That absence, and its counterpart in talk that stresses the importance of moral principles, is traced to the social relations outlined in Chapter 2 under the rubric "Civil Society II." It also coincides with the ontology of actors as set out in Chapter 3, especially with images of the people as herd-like and easy prey for unscrupulous manipulators. Thus, a political role is scripted for altruists to protect the people, even while it is acknowledged by most in the political class that this role is enacted in precisely the opposite way.

Professionalism, a powerful signifier in Russian politics, forms the core of the discourse of competence examined in Chapter 5. The interview narratives indicate that this is, again, a split discourse whose separate dimensions are articulated, respectively, by those who have entered politics from professional careers and those whose careers have been in politics. The former – "professionals in politics" – are represented primarily by the cohorts from the two El'tsin administrations and those from the democratic opposition, while the latter – "professional politicians" – are found among those from the Gorbachev and Putin eras.

Professionals in politics base their claim to power on cultural capital, which for them takes the form of specialized knowledge plus "disinterestedness" – the notion that their activity is governed by the ethics of truth-telling, sincerity and a selfless commitment to social purpose. The term "professional" functions in their narratives as an "empty signifier" engendering group and individual identity even while it erases any notion of interest, let alone advantage-seeking, that professionals might themselves have. The emptiness in question here is evinced by the stories that they tell about their time in government service, which reveal that their prior professional training and experience proved to be little match for the situations that they encountered in political life. Although their confessed ineffectiveness would cancel their claim to power based on specialized knowledge, they redeem that claim by reference to their own professional ethics. This redemption, in turn, derives mainly from their criticism of the other – the professional politician – whom they describe as pridefully cynical, mendacious, thieving, and whose actions make for dirty politics yielding only dirty results.

Whereas professionals in politics embody the cultural capital that represents their claim to power – which means that in political life they are required *to be themselves* – professional politicians, whose claim derives from social and political capital, aver that stance. At critical junctures, they argue, they are required by their profession *not to be themselves*. They must replace moral principles with situational ethics; they favor results over ethical procedures; they rely not on knowledge but on know-how, the ability to come up with creative solutions that harmonize different interests and produce consensus. Know-how represents not specialized knowledge brought to the political world from without, but that "feel for the game" that one develops within it.

Unlike professionals in politics, professional politicians rarely reference particular social purposes that the state is enjoined to pursue. For them, the world does not consist of problems to be solved by application of specialized knowledge. Rather, the world seems a permanently messy place whose problems are there to be managed and where solutions to them are necessarily contingent and imperfect. In certain respects, their version of professional discourse represents an iteration of the core of political discourse itself, the recognition of a particular vocation as described by Max Weber in his essay, referenced, above. Yet embedded in the social relations characteristic of Civil Society *II*, their narratives fall short of including a public in their conception of the political, underscoring the gulf between state and society that persists in Russia.

That gulf is further explored in Chapter 6, which throws into the mix all the elements in the model of political discourse examined separately in the preceding chapters. Here, the discussion turns to respondents' recollections of Russia's recent revolution, inquiring whether their memories and assessments of that event would accord with one another sufficiently to sustain a common narrative on the genesis of the Russian nation-state that might symbolically mediate a foundational tale for the larger political community. The interview responses, however, resist that interpretation, displaying dissension rather than consensus on all principal aspects of the revolution: when it began and ended; what is was about; whether it reached its objectives; and what it has meant for the country's future. This dissension is reflected in a public absence, inasmuch as there remains effectively no commemorative rituals or sites marking either the birth of the state or the labor that brought it to life.

Chapter 6 plumbs the interview narratives for those discursive properties that might explain the lack of agreement within the political class and the concomitant absence of commemoration in the public sphere. At bottom, the findings are twofold. First, disagreement occurs within the ambit of a single discourse. Respondents make no reference to such things as, say, God's will or Russia's destiny that would be inconsistent with any of the narrative programs that surfaced during interviews. Those programs all share a common set of basic categories – so, it appears, the respondents are indeed talking to one another in the same language – but the categories are deployed differently by altering the valences of their core terms. These alterations, in turn, are accomplished through the mediating effect of two binary oppositions that underpin or structure remarks addressed to the topic of revolution: fate/agency and romance/anti-romance. When speaking about the revolution, subjects filter the deeper categories of discourse through these binaries in ways enabling the production of difference and, thus, the taking of positions (dissension) on the field of political communication.

To illustrate this communicative process, there are instances in which subjects refer to the disintegration of the USSR, and to Russia's emergence from it, in terms of fate, an objective fact or process recognized by competent statesmen who achieved optimal (moral) results by averting the calamity of civil war. Against that position, others dismiss the idea of "fate" entirely, arguing that it was not objective circumstances but incompetent and venal power holders who caused the (immoral) loss of their country. "Romance" and "anti-romance" are used in comparable ways. Sometimes the former functions as a halo adorning the heads of revolutionaries or as an alibi for unpleasant consequences said to be beyond their control. Here, competence and morality are conjoined. In other instances, however, competence and morality set off in opposite directions as subjects describe the naiveté of the romantic (incompetent but moral) who has been marginalized in the revolutionary process by unscrupulous (competent but immoral) individuals grabbing power and money for themselves. This move crosses the boundary, turning hope (romance) into disillusionment (anti-romance).

Second, the differences thereby produced within a single discourse map rather closely onto the five cohorts in the sample. Each group approaches uniformity with respect to the ways in which its members construct their respective positions on the matter of revolution. They achieve this result by assigning the same or similar values to the terms in the binaries and, accordingly, draw on discourses of competence and morality to characterize their positions, along the lines of the process illustrated above. The main line of division among them places those in the first and second El'tsin administrations on one side; those in the democratic opposition together with the members of Gorbachev- and Putin-era cohorts on the other. This pattern of position-taking is traced to the distribution of positions made available by the discourse in use. Because community and law – the public dimensions of political discourse – go missing, positions based on claims about, say, the popular actions of the people's duly elected representatives or, conversely, the anti-popular actions of those unduly elected, are not occupied. Instead, the personal dimensions of competence and morality yield a more restricted field, bounded by assertions on the order of "We saw what had to be done and we did the right thing," on one hand, and by their imprecating mirror images, on the other.

2 Social relations

> The level of trust that we have today is at the level of the plinth.
> No one trusts anyone (C7).

Most attempts by Western scholars to conceptualize social relations in post-communist countries have fallen under the rubric "civil society." In their interpretation, civil society would represent primarily, if not exclusively, the sphere of voluntary associations thought to bridge the gap between citizens and state. In this version of the concept, the involvement of citizens in society's associational life is valued for breeding the habits and skills of cooperation necessary for common endeavors. In so doing, participation in voluntary associations, it is claimed, produces a generalized "social capital" consisting of high levels of interpersonal trust and tolerance that lubricates the engine of social cooperation and contributes thereby to citizen participation in democratic government (Diamond, 1994).[1]

Perhaps taking their cue from opponents of communist regimes who had boldly inscribed "civil society" on their banners, many of those with an interest in studying – and, perhaps, even assisting in the building of – democracy in the newly liberated states have relied on this conception of civil society to chart the progress of individual states toward democratic futures. The results of these efforts have been disappointing. On the one hand, civil society conceived in this fashion can scarcely be said to exist in post-communist countries, which stand out for recording the lowest levels of citizen participation in voluntary associations among all countries on the globe (Howard, 2003; Hann, 2002). Russia fits squarely into this pattern (Henderson, 2003; Sundstrom, 2006), suggesting that the study of civil society in that country has amounted to examining something

[1] For a very different interpretation of "civil society," more plausibly related to post-communist states, see Ekiert and Kubik (1999) and Kubik (2005).

that is – with rare exception – not to be found, while simultaneously neglecting extant social relations in this quarter of the world. This has led to the unfortunate tendency "to criticize Russian civil society for its [alleged] weakness, fragmentation or even non-existence" and to leave the matter at that (Schmidt-Pfister, 2008: 41). On the other hand, the application of this notion of civil society to post-communist states has produced such confusion and conflation of categories that one student of the subject concludes her extensive review of existing scholarship with the recommendation that this version of "civil society" is sufficiently feckless to warrant its complete exclusion from the post-communist scholarly agenda (Mihaylova, 2004).

What went wrong? Here, I want to explore that question on two levels: (1) by examining the sources of the concept "civil society" itself, showing that from among a variety of differing formulations Western scholars have selected the one that appears to be especially ill-suited to their expressed purposes; and (2) by revealing how the very tradition from which they have chosen to draw that concept has been truncated and misrepresented in ways that all but guarantee a misunderstanding of its purported object. For the sake of convenience, as well as to avoid the inappropriate normative dimension that has accompanied the term, I call the conventional conception "Civil Society I," contrasting it, below, to what may be a more promising formulation, "Civil Society II." Although my remarks might raise questions about the scholarly utility of Civil Society I per se, the question of whether this model corresponds in meaningful ways to social-political relations anywhere is beyond the scope of this study. As such, I will bracket that issue and simply assume that the most robust representation of Civil Society I is found in advanced capitalist democracies. That assumption is purely instrumental. Its purpose is to set up a contrast with Civil Society II that serves as a point of departure for investigating social-political relations in Russia. After sketching those relations, attention then turns to the interview narratives which put some meat on the bones of the model.

SOURCES OF THE CONCEPT "CIVIL SOCIETY"

Western scholars began employing the term "civil society" to capture what were thought to be key aspects of social and political relations in the USSR even before communism had collapsed (Starr, 1989; Bova, 1991; Lapidus, 1991; Wiegle and Butterfield, 1992). In this respect, they seemed to be following the lead of some of communism's most articulate opponents in Eastern Europe who had deployed this idea against their respective regimes to great political effect (Havel, 1985; Michnik, 1985). Indeed, at the beginning of the twentieth century's final decade, one scholar observed that "the two most powerful concepts in the political vocabulary of Eastern Europe are those of 'civil society' and 'citizenship'" (Kolankiewicz, 1992: 142). The moral-political edge for "civil society" honed by East European intellectuals no doubt accounted for the concept's attractiveness not only to domestic supporters, but to many Western intellectuals and governments, as well as to donor organizations abroad. It may be that this moral-political dimension, so useful to their project of ridding their societies of communism and justifying the neo-liberal agenda of the intelligentsia in communism's wake (Eyal, Szelenyi and Townsley, 1998) masked the fact that the concept itself had neither a practical-political orientation nor much scholarly purchase. As John Ehrenberg (1999: 196) has remarked, "a 'self-governing' civil society with no professional political parties, autonomous political bodies, or institutionalized political life was a fantasy from the very beginning." Accordingly, as the focus of attention turned from opposition to communism toward the actual issues of politics and government in communism's aftermath, "civil society" quickly disappeared from the political lexicon of post-communist countries (Lomax, 1997), except on rare occasions when it was revived for purely polemical purposes (Myant, 2005).

Although the air had quickly gone out of the civil-society balloon across post-communist political space, the reverse appears to have been true for many scholars and those working for donor agencies in the West who adjusted their research and funding programs to study and build civil societies there. Particularly for political scientists in the United States, the civil-society vogue of the 1980s and 1990s appeared to resuscitate the seminal conventions of pluralism and "civic culture" (Almond and Verba, 1963) whose once prominent position on the intellectual map of their discipline had been displaced by new approaches promising greater rigor and more cumulative results (Baumgartner and Leech, 1998). Within this context, Robert Putnam's *Making Democracy Work* (1993) could scarcely have been more timely for elaborating the rationale for what I am calling Civil Society *I*, linking it to the democratic project under way in most of the post-communist world. Putnam's study of regional government performance in Italy purported to show via both historical and survey analysis that government worked best where there were longstanding civic traditions of participation in voluntary associations that yielded the social capital necessary to sustain collective action and generate cooperative relations between citizens and the state. The book thus joined the normative desiderata of citizen involvement and democracy to the practical concern for governmental effectiveness, anchoring this union in extensive empirical research and producing thereby a synthesis that seemed to provide a solid social science basis for the more speculative civil-society orientation that had been offered by East European intellectuals. In my view, the answer to the question – What went wrong? – is bound up, above all, with the reception and application of Putnam's ideas. Therefore, I will unpack them a bit, here.

First, there is the matter of pedigree. Putnam (1993:171; 2001: 19–20) has maintained that he derived his concept of social capital primarily from James Coleman's (1990) *Foundations of Social Theory*, but there are serious problems attending this claim. One concerns Coleman's theory itself in which two forms of social interaction – interpersonal trust and obligations based on face-to-face relations (particular) and norms that govern the action of all (generalized) – are lumped together under the heading of "social capital" (Coleman, 1990: 320). I shall revisit this lack of distinction below, with reference to Civil Society *II*. Here, I want to call attention to the fact that Putnam's (1993) argument relies entirely on the second type of social capital (generalized) and treats the first type (particular) merely as a supposed generator of the second. *Making Democracy Work* offers no explanation for this move from exclusive forms of social capital (particular) to inclusive forms (generalized). Subsequently, Putnam (2001: 446) has in part recognized this inconsistency, but that recognition has not altered his view of general norms arising from face-to-face interactions that are closely related to civic virtue (2001: 18–19). Consequently, whereas Coleman's conception portrays social capital as an aspect of *social structure* capable of facilitating interaction, cooperation and exchange in concrete and diverse instances, Putnam's detaches social capital from its context and treats it as a universal that can be measured by surveying the opinions, values and other properties or characteristics of *individuals*. Coleman's term is thus emptied of its sociological content and refilled with a kind of essentialism at home with the "civic culture" tradition in which the individual – here, his/her attitudes and opinions – appears as the unit of analysis, and society as the mere aggregate of these individuals evincing qualities such as trust, tolerance and the like. Putnam's claim that particularistic forms of social capital engender generalized feelings of civic-mindedness appears to be predicated on this methodological slip which effectively erases the difference between these two varieties of social capital (Foley and Edwards, 1998b) in favor of an abstract universalist form. However, that very slip has recommended Putnam's conception to many students of civil society inasmuch as, in addition to universalizing the concept and thus making it portable to any location, it provides a definite empirical referent (voluntary associations, albeit shorn of context) and a clear set of indicators for measurement: individual values, attitudes, and so on (Newton, 1997; Foley and Edwards, 1997b).

To this analytic orientation derived from his revisions of Coleman's concept of social capital, Putnam has added a normative dimension appropriated from Alexis de Tocqueville's classic, *Democracy in America*. This move involves two reductions that supply his civil society with mythic significance, projecting an image of the good society, one composed of a participant citizenry harmoniously joined together in the pursuit of the common good, while simultaneously improving themselves in Tocqueville's "great free schools of association." The first reduction had been carried out by Tocqueville himself, who abstracted his concept of civil society from the economic relations in which its members were embedded. Consequently, whereas thinkers such as Hegel or Madison – who included the economy in their theories of civic association – had portrayed civil society as a site of conflict, for Tocqueville it would be one of cooperation. The second reduction, Putnam's, takes the matter a step further by ignoring the issues of freedom and equality that did concern Tocqueville and led him to problematize his account by introducing his notion of "tyranny of the majority" and linking it to political power and the state. These issues go missing in Putnam's account (Foley and Edwards, 1997a). Consequently, this twofold reduction yields a civil society that is not only decontextualized but apolitical (Tarrow, 1996; Rothstein, 2004). As such, it is fitted to the task of supplying that moral underpinning that has appeared to have made it particularly attractive to scholars concerned with its (re)emergence and to donor agencies intent on building it (Carothers and Ottaway, 2000; Ehrenberg, 1999: 233–234).

This depoliticized concept of civil society can, however, perform certain political functions. One involves supplying the rationale for governmental and corporate support to nongovernmental organizations (NGOs) – to which "civic associations" are usually reduced in practice – as a part of the neo-liberal strategy for shrinking the state while simultaneously building democracy (Aksartova, 2005; Seligman, 2002; Foley and Edwards, 1998a). However, with respect to democracy, the evidence seems to point in the opposite direction for post-communist countries (Quigley, 2000; Henderson, 2003; and for Latin America, Encarnacion, 2003).

Another function involves the imposition of good guy/bad guy distinctions in the face of civic associations of which the observer does not approve. Although historical surveys of extant civil societies have shown that the individual and collective impact of voluntary associations on the polity have often enough led to anti-democratic outcomes favoring nationalist-authoritarian versions of class rule (Bermeo and Nord, 2000), those adhering to the Civil Society *I* paradigm tend to overlook such instances in order to sustain the allegedly democratic effect of civic associations.[2] When that effect does not occur, theoretic interests give way to normative ones distinguishing bad associations from good ones, the ones granted admission to civil society by the analyst. Putnam's (2001: 22) example of the Ku Klux Klan's plan to adopt a Florida highway would be a case in point. Characterizing this episode, Putnam abruptly drops his own position regarding civic engagement generating the virtues of trust and tolerance. Instead, he substitutes the image of bad people seeking to dupe others by putting on a show of public-spiritedness.

Similar instances of this denigration of the other can be found in the literature on civil society in post-communist countries. Surveying the situation in Russia, one scholar laments the ample presence there of what he calls "antimodern social capital" while another concerned with Albania has characterized that society as in the throes of "primitive social capital" (Mihaylova, 2004: 25–26, 125). Inasmuch as this discourse of civil society contains what Alvin Gouldner (1985) has referred to as a "paleosymbolic level" of communication – one whose obscurity on the surface makes it all the more powerful for conveying deep ideological categories – it tends to celebrate a notion of the good society in which "people like us" participate. Accordingly, it can serve as tacit warrant for denying the imprimatur of civil society to places in which civic associations indeed exist, simply because the communist party enjoys sizeable voter support there (Marsh, 2000). In this respect proponents of Civil Society *I* too often continue the practices of pronouncing judgment on allegedly miscreant citizens – such as Havel's (1985) morally

---

[2] Perhaps the premier instance of a vibrant civil society engendering nationalist-authoritarian politics would be the case of Weimar Germany (Berman, 1997). On the pitfalls of the civil-society model generally, see Encarnacion (2006).

deficient greengrocer or Michnik's (1985: 152) disappointment with "the passivity, lack of courage, and the general absence of social consciousness on the part of the workers as a whole" – and thus by implication normatively valorizing themselves as superior persons inhabiting a superior social order. The same counts for social relations themselves, whereby those involving weak ties (Granovetter, 1973) are regarded as more eufunctional than those marked by strong ones (Putnam, 2001: 22–23).

These normative distinctions drawn by proponents of the prevailing model of civil society appear to implicate them in the very object of their study. Particularly if viewed through the lens of Antonio Gramsci's (1971) theory of class hegemony operating through the institutions of civil society itself – educational institutions, publishing, donor organizations and so on – a disturbing picture emerges of a multi-billion dollar "non-profit industrial complex" (Rodriguez, 2007) actively engaged in the support and defense internationally of existing patterns of social, economic and political power. Individual intentions are not at issue, here. Rather, at stake are the actual effects of that complex whose operations are couched in the language of "civil society" and "social capital" (Guilhot, 2005). For conventional civil-society proponents in the West, one such effect would seem to follow from discursive strategies identified by Teun van Dijk (2006) that underscore "Our good things" versus "Their bad things." In this instance, the conventional concept of civil societies serves as justification for the putative social order in which Westerners live, while pointing to its absence elsewhere not only reminds them of their good fortune but of their assumed duty to share it with others.

To sum up thus far: the concepts of civil society and social capital currently in vogue among Western scholars are ill suited to the task of analyzing social and political relations in post-communist Russia. Empirically, they are weakly represented in the actual associative life of Russian society, thus amounting to an injunction to study that which is not much present, but somehow should be. From the standpoint of theory, these concepts are problematic in a number of ways:

particularistic social capital is not meaningfully distinguished from its generalized form and an unwarranted assumption is made that the particularistic version produces the generalized variety; social capital as a concept in use has been detached from social structure and converted into an abstract universal to be discovered in the characteristics of individuals; civil society has been depoliticized and there is little sensitivity to the role of the state in structuring it; and the concepts have acquired an inappropriate moral content that prejudices the view of observers and distorts their vision.

Finally, I want to question the theoretic utility of the concept of generalized social capital that is congruent with the "civic culture" tradition inaugurated by US scholars. The notion of generalized social capital lacks precision. That is, the term "capital" is used in a purely metaphorical sense, shorn of the notions of power and the individual appropriation of the resources or labor of others that have long accompanied its usage in scholarly discourse. As such, the empirical interpretation of the concept remains amorphous. Rather than specific stocks of social capital at the disposal of individuals who deploy them in social interaction, this notion constructs some common larder of social capital from which individuals freely draw. Such a conception departs from the meaning and theoretical import of the noun, "capital." Voluntary cooperation has replaced, in this conception, the problematic of power, its production, deployment and reproduction. Moreover, at the core of "capital" – as Karl Marx observed long ago – is not a thing but a social relation. Accordingly, there seems small purpose in treating "social capital" as a measurable individual characteristic connoting a propensity to trust unfamiliar others. Rather the utility of "capital" issues from social interaction and exchange. That is where "it" is present in a meaningful sense, in its disappearance and conversion into something else, especially into other forms of capital.

FORMS OF CAPITAL: FORMS OF CIVIL SOCIETY

Among contemporary thinkers engaged with the concept "capital" the work of Pierre Bourdieu has been seminal. In a general sense, he has followed the Marxist tradition, conceptualizing capital as "accumulated labor" that is "appropriated on a private, i.e., exclusive, basis by agents or groups of agents, enabling them to appropriate social energy ... [It is] the principle underlying the immanent regularities of the social world" (Bourdieu, 1986: 241). However, Bourdieu has also revolutionized that perspective, theorizing capital as a relation taking one of three basic forms: economic, cultural and social. The first of these represents that which has been instituted by property rights and can be directly converted into money. It is a possession standing apart from its possessor and, thus, appears as *disembodied*. The same is not true of the other two forms which appear, correspondingly, as *embodied* capital. Cultural capital is accumulated by work on the self in accordance with some socially instituted value. It is produced above all by the educational system, but not only by it. It amounts to converting forms of external wealth – say, knowledge, or the capacity to produce cultural goods such as a work of art – into an integral part of the person who embodies this capital itself. The value of this capital increases in proportion to its exclusivity. Likewise, social capital is both embodied and unevenly distributed. It appears as the aggregate resources on which an individual can draw owing to her place within a social network. This form of capital involves social ties, reciprocity and mutual aid. Holders of this type of capital acquire a particular status, whether formally or informally acknowledged, that can command the resources and energies of others. In short, it too is a form of power. And like the other forms of capital, it can be converted into the other forms themselves: say, acquiring a high-paying job through friendship connections (Bourdieu, 1984, 1986, 1990, 1993). Bourdieu's forms of capital – and their particular mix in a given instance – can be regarded as a deep structure of social relations, that bedrock on which institutions are constructed.

For my purposes, the relevance of this conception consists in its utility, from a reasonably high level of abstraction, to distinguish social relations presupposed in Western models of civil society (Civil Society *I*), where economic capital is dominant, from social relations in Russia where cultural and social capital play the major roles. By

Table 2.1 *Two models of civil society*

	Civil Society *I*	Civil Society *II*
Dominant organizational form	civic associations	informal networks
Dominant form of capital	economic	cultural or (embodied) social
Strength of ties among actors	weak	strong
Focus of collective action	specific	diffuse
Social capital	generalized, disembodied	particularized, embodied
State	strong (rule of law)	weak (personal appropriation of public offices)

historically grounding the concept of civil society (Burawoy, 2004; Jameson, 1998) in this way, ideal types can be developed that counterpose two very different social logics corresponding to their respective mixes of capitals.[3] As depicted in Table 2.1, Civil Society *I* (the Western pattern) would be characterized by "weak" social ties among the members of civic associations (Granovetter, 1973, 1982) whose collective action is fixed on specific purposes. The product of social interaction would be *generalized* social capital which, in turn, would require the impersonality of a strong state maintaining a rule of law. In counter-distinction to this pattern, Civil Society *II* (the Russian pattern) would feature "strong" ties amounting to an affective involvement among the parties to interaction (Granovetter, 1973, 1982)

---

[3] It goes without saying that ideal types cannot be regarded as empirical models. As such, there may well be a presence of the elements associated with Civil Society *II* in countries characterized as belonging to Civil Society *I*, and conversely. The use of ideal types represents an analytical choice justified by the *degree* to which it fits one or another empirical instance.

whose purposes are multiform or "diffuse." The social capital accumulated by parties in interaction would be particular or embodied. It does not so much lubricate the engine of social cooperation as sustain the existence of diffuse social networks of mutual aid for whom general social purposes remain, at best, matters of indifference. This arrangement would be, in turn, predicated on the existence of a weak state unable to enforce impersonal rules, of which the pattern itself is both cause and consequence. On one hand, the absence of the rule of law tends to encourage social interaction based on high levels of particularistic personal trust that appear to outsiders as corruption. For the participants themselves, however, these patterns are regarded matter-of-factly as essential to the accomplishment of common purposes. Because of the affective valence that commonly accompanies these relationships, they can figure directly in identity formation, contributing to the ongoing reproduction of "us" (Ledenova, 2004a). On the other hand, within this milieu, the rule of law is itself marginalized. Even in cases in which, say, courts are actually fulfilling their function as an independent arbiter of disputes, recourse to their auspices can be seen as a form of betrayal, as calling on "them" and thereby destroying the possibility that "we" might resolve the conflict. Turning to the state to adjudicate disputes may thus appear as an immoral attempt "to break somebody down" (Radaev, 2004: 96).

Some scholars concerned with post-communist transitions in Eastern Europe have profitably deployed Bourdieu's forms of capital to explain otherwise perplexing features of the transitions themselves (Derluguian, 2003; Eyal, Szelenyi and Townsley, 1998; Zarycki, 2003). Following their lead, I want to use Bourdieu's forms of capital to explain the prevalence of patterns associated with Civil Society *II* in the Russian case. The conventional concept of civil society, Civil Society *I*, is predicated on the dominant role of economic capital. Because it is disembodied, societies structured primarily by this form of capital admit to the generation of abstract categories (citizen) and impersonal procedures (the rule of law) which occlude real differences that obtain among individuals with respect to their access to, and possession of, economic, cultural and social capital. As such, individuals confront one another in the public sphere as equals, as citizens. That equality presents itself as a basic condition for association in voluntary groups (Walzer, 2002). And while the varieties of capital no doubt have a powerful influence on both the internal life and external capabilities of these associations, they do not enter directly in their constitution, which remains "voluntary": that is, presupposing both impersonal procedures and the formal equality of members.

This pattern is reversed when either cultural or (embodied) social capital is dominant. In such instances, *embodied* capital, unequally distributed, figures directly into the constitutive process. The terrain of association, so to speak, is not level. Individuals encounter one another as immediately unequal in their possession of these embodied forms of capital which structure relations within associations in unequal ways. Rather than joining a voluntary association composed of peers, one either participates in a closed network of informal exchange, structured by varying degrees of social capital among its members that often generate clientelistic practices, or in associations whose structures consist of hierarchies defined by their members' embodiment of cultural capital. In the first instance, social trust is confined to circles of mutual aid and patronage relations whose "particularized trust has been developed in opposition to universalized *dis*trust" (Shevchenko, 2008: 169, italics in original). In the second, it is placed – usually from a distance – in those regarded as "better than us." In either case, the generalized social capital attendant on Civil Society *I* gives way to the opposing pattern of Civil Society *II*.

This discussion of civil society throws the matter of political organization into sharp relief. If political parties and interest associations are forms of organization congruent with the social relations common to Civil Society *I*, then an altogether different pattern is consistent with the forms found in Civil Society *II*. There, social relations are reticulated in network structures based on strong ties and particularized social capital. They organize collective action in diffuse ways that contribute to the needs satisfaction of their various members located in a variety of social positions. When these networks – owing to the location of at least some of their members in governmental hierarchies – have access to state power, they can be regarded as "power networks" with the capacity to subvert the formal institutions of state and society (Afanas'ev, 2000; Volkov, 2002; Hayoz and Sergeyev, 2003; Mbeke, 2001). Thus, executive agencies, political parties and interest associations operating within the set of social relations characteristic of Civil Society *II* appear as weak institutions composed of one or more power networks that supply them with impulse, direction and purpose (Urban, 2003). Where do these networks come from and how are they structured?

It appears that two conditions have accounted for the emergence of power networks as the dominant form of political association in Russia. The first is traceable to the supersession of property rights by administrative rights under the old (socialist) order (Verdery, 1996, 2003). To the degree that the control of administrative office awarded to individuals and cliques the ability to control the disposition of material and social resources more or less irrespective of formal regulations (Urban, 1985, 1989, 1997), embodied capitals of the cultural and social variety infused society's institutions with a decidedly personalized element. Second, patterns of collective responsibility – and, in reaction to them, informal, collusive modes of collective self-defense – imposed during tsarist times were often continued under new names during the Soviet period (Hosking, 2004; Ledeneva, 2004b: 2006). Thus, the ritualized forms of social organization characteristic of the Soviet order often spilled over into the private sphere where they permutated into friendship networks whose thick relationships anchored individuals in tight circles of familiar others (Kharkhordin, 1998, 2000; Urban, 2004). These Soviet-era networks provided the initial basis for organizing in the late- and post-Soviet periods, reticulating themselves outward through the patronage of their members in control of both state and non-state offices, thereby developing over time into extended networks of power that in at least some instances have shown a tendency toward transforming themselves into vertically organized patronage structures (Kharkhordin, 2009a).

As has been observed in the instances of many post-communist countries, power networks congeal as exchange media connecting members in possession of state offices with their partners occupying important positions in the economy (Verdery, 1996; Greskovits, 1998; Stark, 1997; Stark and Bruszt, 1998). Consequently, these ties enable power networks – taken collectively and in competition with one another – to orchestrate the activities of both state and economy. Access to desired resources is the critical desideratum, and access, in turn, depends either upon bribes to outsiders (state officials or agents of organized crime) or, when state offices are included in the network, upon strong ties to one's network partners (Djankov *et al.*, 2004). In restrained language, Russia's president, Dmitrii Medvedev, has himself called public attention to these patterns, noting that "decisions on placing people to official positions are sometimes taken through the buddy system – along the principle of personal loyalty or, what's more disgusting, for money when positions are kind of sold" (Itar-Tass, 2008). Moreover, even when exchange transcends the domestic economy, as in the instance of foreign direct investment, these network structures appear to be determinant (Bandelj, 2002; Stark and Vedres, 2006).

In broad strokes, power-network structures tend to assume two forms. The first, which passes in Russian parlance under the pejorative "clans" (*klany*), usually involves both a core of people who are longstanding acquaintances who remain connected despite differing official affiliations (Wedel, 2005) and a peripheral membership comprised of individuals who developed ties with the core members once the core group had become ensconced in public offices, dispensing patronage and recruiting new allies (Flap and Volker, 2003; Hayoz and Sergeyev, 2003). One of the respondents in the present survey described power-network structure and formation in this way:

> For moving upward, it is always essential to establish your own
> personal network. It's absolutely necessary. In the conditions of

soft authoritarianism under which we live, a person must braid together as many personal ties as possible with all representatives of power. The dynamics of your career depend most of all on personal contacts, on establishing friendly, informal contacts with a huge number of people. That's how a new person enters and begins to ascend the ladder. But further on, a clan will draw you in. The access that weak ties have provided you becomes a resource that you can offer to one or another clan. To the extent that a clan then swallows you up, they require your loyalty. The higher you rise within the clan, naturally, the more your ties to others wither away. [They had been serviceable] in getting you noticed and without them no one will give you a break. They don't even see you ... But once you have begun to move up within a certain clan, then your career will depend exclusively on so-called strong contacts (C6).

Janine Wedel (1998) encountered just such a power network on the receiving end of Western assistance to Russia. Working through state and non-state bodies, core members appropriated foreign funds and expertise, applying them directly to their personal enrichment, network objectives and the recruitment of new members. As Wedel observed, the core group constituted a single, collective actor. Furthermore, it appears that network recruitment has begun to take a more regularized form as the control of credentialing institutions for work in the state sector has increasingly fallen to power networks, thus building patronage relations directly into the process by which the civil service is constituted (Huskey, 2004).

That tendency has been further strengthened by civil service reforms that have relocated the personnel function in government away from executive agencies and concentrated it more in the Administration of the President. One consequence of these changes has been the attenuation of vertical mobility within the hierarchies of government offices and the concomitant acceleration of lateral entries into top state jobs (Huskey, 2005). This has enabled power networks associated with the former president, Vladimir Putin, to seize the commanding heights of office in the state (Kryshtanovskaya, 2005) and to take control of the key sectors of Russia's economy (Volkov, 2008). Another result of civil service reform has resembled a reconstruction of the Soviet system of job appointments, the *nomenklatura*, whereby centralized lists of "reserve cadres" are composed by the Administration of the President's personnel department (*Upravlenie kadrov*) for future work not only in government, but for leading positions in business firms and NGOs. In selecting from these lists, senior officials avoid legal requirements for filling vacancies on a competitive basis, thus extending patron–client relations in their organizations (Huskey, 2005), a practice that had been every bit as much a part of the Soviet order as had been the *nomenklatura* (Willerton, 1992; Urban, 1989; Rigby and Harasymiw, 1983).

A respondent spoke at considerable length about the consequences of this pattern for Russia's society and economy, instantiating the collusion between Western-based transnational capital and domestic trade-financial groups with headquarters in the executive. Estimating losses to country as running into many billions of dollars, he argued that:

> When goals [in politics] are principally personal enrichment, then the means are chicanery and intrigue ... The flock can only count on its own shepherd if the shepherd is required to care for the flock. But if the shepherd has reached agreement with both the other shepherds and the wolves, then he will throw the flock to the wolves with pleasure ... We have authoritarian power, not personally Putin's but that of a group ... obediently associated with more powerful Western forces. Hence, they are not concerned [with developing] the country's productive potential. They are involved in trade and finance and conduct themselves, as Tocqueville would have it, as trade-finance [groups]. For us, this means searching for and supporting those forms [of association that can] restrict the Rothschilds. Otherwise, our economy becomes a casino and society is degraded even further (*D2*).

Although a moral tone suffuses his remarks, it is also clear that he attributes this outcome not to the shortcomings of individuals but to the relations in which they are embedded – hence, his call for new forms of association.

Especially since the advent of Vladimir Putin, the personnel function performed by the Administration of the President has taken on a decidedly clientelistic character, explaining why so many of Putin's confederates from his careers in the KGB and in St. Petersburg's municipal government – "he even remembers to appoint his former schoolmates to one or another post" as one respondent noted (D4) – now chair the boards of directors of the country's industrial and financial giants (Kryshtanovskaya, 2005; Kryshtanovskaya and White, 2005; Fazullina, 2004; Makarkin, 2004), while their relatives and associates are appointed to top jobs in ostensibly private firms doing business with the government (Anon., 2005). However, while Putin might represent the country's grand patron, the current arrangement also conduces to competition and conflict among clientelist groups, even at the top of the power hierarchy (Salin, 2007; Kryshtanovskaya, 2005; Pribylovskii, 2005). Not only do grandees jockey for position and access to power and money, but the veiled nature of this competition means for the participants themselves that things are far from clear, stable, or predictable. As one respondent, drawing on his own experience, remarked:

> Everything transpires through groups of people, groups of interests. In a stable society you know these groups of people. But in our country unanticipated groups might arise, unanticipated teams or sub-teams that seek their own private interests. And these interests can collide with your sense of things [otsenkami]. In principle, all teams act within the frameworks of regimes, which is completely understandable, and usually the direction of their politics is known. But if some teams appear whose political direction is unknown, then this is always a complicated phenomenon (E2).

This respondent's reference to "teams" (*komandy*) represents the other broad category into which power networks might fall. It tends to function as the polite form for denominating these groupings, and in the interview sample it is regularly used to denote one's own network. The pejorative form – "clans" – is more often reserved for networks with which one is not directly associated. To be sure, in this context, both terms are used metaphorically. For instance, "clans" does not connote kin relations. Rather, the term's significance seems to be derived from two background understandings present among Russian political actors, one of which would be culturally proximate but remote in time, the other, culturally remote but contemporary. The first refers to centuries of the country's political history in which clans comprised the sinews of the tsarist state. Clan activity was based on strong bonds of loyalty, while the set of relations among clans was governed by strict rules of protocol, codes of honor and conduct, and amounted to de facto claims on appointments to state offices (Kollmann, 1987, 1999; Keenan, 1986). In this respect, "clans" taps into cultural relevance, referencing a form of association in which similarly strong bonds within networks fused their members into collective actors and structured internal relations within each grouping according to hierarchical patterns of fealty and patronage. The second connotation alludes to the Soviet successor states of Central Asia, where clan relations *qua* kinship networks had operated as the controlling force in politics throughout the Soviet period – despite Moscow's concerted efforts to neutralize them – and continue to do so today (Roy, 2000; Schatz, 2004). This aspect of the metaphor suggests comparison to an other, once a part of a common state, which is subject to broad cultural denigration in Russia as odiously backward and uncivilized. Thus, at the vortex of these two background understandings, the metaphor of clans had been fashioned as a signifier in Russian political discourse during the 1990s, referring initially to a partially kin-based grouping (widely regarded as especially corrupt) that appeared to hold a determining share of power in the Russian state – the power network arrayed around President

Boris El'tsin, "the Family" – and was subsequently generalized to all power groupings (also seen as corrupt) operating throughout the state and economy. In the prevailing political vernacular, then, "clans" signifies the illicit power of tightly bound groups of confederates who have already seized all that is worth seizing even while the seizing from one another still goes on (Barnes, 2006).

Likewise, "teams" is a metaphor primarily drawn from the world of sport. It tends to connote a set of relations based on functional proficiencies joined in collective effort – "teamwork" – and infused with a spirit of collegiality. Thus, the distinction dawn by respondents between "clans" and "teams" can be put to analytic, rather than simply invidious, purpose. That is, while "clans" refer to the sort of personalized configurations hitherto described, "teams" are more loosely structured, localized and focused on some project, however vaguely formulated, that defines their collective purpose. As a sociocultural phenomenon, teams bind together their members on the basis of familiarity, a form of "intimacy without warmth, automatically extended and received as soon as the individual takes a place on the team" (Goffman, 1973: 83). Yet, insofar as teams develop their own identities, their goals tend to reflect a degree of ambiguity. This allows for both an integration of members around the symbolic mediation of the goals themselves while, at the same time, it opens up space for individual maneuver, project redefinition and the meeting of unanticipated exigencies that accommodates extended interaction (White, 1992). These descriptors seem to fit the phenomenon of teams in Russia (Daugavet, 2003), but cultural proclivities there may award – as articulated by respondents, below – a larger role to affect. Like clans, teams tend to produce a very restricted "we," leaving no place in elite discourse for the generation of larger identities related to social standing or even to the organizations in which teams function. Unlike the patterns attributed to Civil Society *I*, the articulation of identities publicly is severely restricted for power networks, thus foreclosing the possibilities of extended social or political cooperation at root level. In Civil Society *II*, social differentiation is not symbolically mediated. Outside of tit-for-tat deals done on an ad hoc basis, insiders neither have need of others nor are there identifiable (collective) others whose cooperation they might solicit.

CLANS AND TEAMS IN THE CONSCIOUSNESS OF POLITICAL ACTORS

Although a more complete elaboration of the significance of the social relations just sketched is the topic of subsequent chapters, it remains here to tap into the body of interview narratives in order to record how subjects reflect on the role of personal connections characteristic of Civil Society *II* in their own political experience. Their comments are organized around three aspects of the model in which personalized relations figure directly: recruitment to government offices, clans and teams.

Recruitment. A number of respondents brought up their recruitment to government jobs – although they were not asked about this. With the partial exception of a particular team formed during the second El'tsin administration,[4] personal ties to the occupants of government offices were directly involved. In most cases, their descriptions of recruitment were simple and direct. "I had been working for a journal with Egor Gaidar," remarked one (*C2*),

> and when he became acting prime minister I transferred over to his team.
>
> Question: *How did that happen?*
> C2:   I was looking for work. I then was working as a political observer for TASS and my relations with the directors were not very good. I simply came [to Gaidar] and said that I'm ready to work.
> Question: *Seriously?*
> C2:   We always had good relations.
> Question: *Were these personal relations with Gaidar?*
> C2:   Not deeply personal. Well, I was an acquaintance of his family. So our relations were partly professional and partly personal.

---

[4] See Chapter 5.

In other instances, the process was more circuitous. One official discussed at great length – over 30 minutes – his recruitment into the Gorbachev administration, recounting a labyrinth of personal and professional connections that he had developed with fellow academics working in it that eventually led to his appointment as Deputy Minister for the Environment. Following the failed putsch of August 1991, some of these contacts proved useful in landing him a ministerial post in El'tsin's government.

> I had some contacts with [Aleksandr] Shokhin and Gaidar who met with me in September–October. Around the end of October, one of them rang – I think it was Shokhin and not Gaidar – and said: Viktor Ivanovich, can you come to Sosenki [a state dacha where many in the soon-to-be appointed government were residing – M. U.]? I said, "And why not? Of course I can, I know the road." They told me that they were forming a new government of the Russian Federation and asked me to join it as Minister for the Environment and Natural Resources ... I agreed and then returned to my position in the all-union ministry ... It was rather amusing there on the following day when a meeting was called by [Nikolai] Vorontsov [the Minister – M. U.] who was conjecturing, while we sat in his office, about which of us would be appointed to the government being formed by El'tsin. Those present discussed from their points of view whom might be appointed and nobody named me. Well, I was quietly laughing to myself, observing this circus. A few days later, El'tsin signed the decree designating me as minister (B3).

Others, however, took a less charitable view of the process of recruitment via personal connections. For example, another member of the Gaidar reform team had this to say:

> Personal relationships play an enormous role. I never joined any clan, being already close to the reform leaders [vozhdyam] and sufficiently prickly that I couldn't do anything but express my own [contrary] opinions. I remained independent and stubborn, even

though my family would have been enormously glad if it were otherwise ... But I participated in many aspects of the reforms, and I saw two groups of people who succeeded in enriching themselves. One was that part of the [old] *nomenklatura* who had come over to El'tsin to establish their control over the country, particularly in the privatization process. The second group were those who did not bear the weight of excessive achievements. These people were in their twenties and thirties ... For them as well, personal relations played a very big role. In distinction from the East, where clans are composed of family members, here it is friendship relations that [make up] clans (*B1*).

Unlike their counterparts from pervious administrations, those in the Putin cohort rarely raised the issue of recruitment through personal channels. When they did, it was either to disclaim participation in it (*E5*) or to refer obliquely to an unremarkable process (*E2*).

Clans. As noted, above, "clans" surfaced during interviews frequently, pejoratively and invariably in reference to others. When comparable phenomena pertaining to one's group were under discussion, either a softer edge or altogether different terms would be used, as illustrated by these remarks:

- Boris El'tsin worked for a long time with Oleg Lobov in the Sverdlovsk obkom [Communist Party regional leadership – M.U.] where they solved political and economic problems. Then they repeated this experience in Moscow, El'tsin as president and Lobov as a minister ... In addition to these relations of office, however, there are informal relations, above all *zemlyachestvo* [people from the same region – M. U.]. So, in this particular case, when the president issued a directive, it would be not merely a presidential directive but a directive from someone close to the recipient, someone who is from the same region, someone who shares a background with the president himself. And, of course, El'tsin knows this when he issues the directive. On each side there is a certain trust in the other, not to mention the fact that, in this case, the recipient, Lobov, had built up a relationship of trust with

El'tsin over a long period ... Each party regarded the other as comrade-*zemlyak* ... But it's not so simple because there was only one *zemlyak* among the assistants to the president: Viktor Ilyushin. All the rest were Muscovites. So the Administration of the President did not become a clan, a *zemlyachestvo* of people from Sverdlovsk (*C1*).

• It was always characteristic for the Soviet *nomenklatura* [officialdom – M. U.] to surround themselves with people coming from their same regional clans. And this was true of El'tsin, too. Unconditionally. But he nonetheless included others in his government who had no relation to the *nomenklatura* or to Sverdlovsk ... And I can say with certitude that neither under Soviet power, nor under El'tsin in his early or late period, were members of a clan so dense a crowd surrounding the throne as they are now in the person, so to speak, of the *chekists* [secret police – M. U.] and Petersburgers (*B9*).

Although the El'tsin presidency was notorious for the highly personalized, clannish relations surrounding it (Breslauer, 2001), these remarks from two of its members tend to minimize this characteristic when it comes to describing their own experience. Nonetheless, as the second set of comments indicates, they are somewhat less generous when referring to comparable phenomena detected among others.[5] Indeed, when viewing the behavior of others in the light of their personal networks, respondents collectively composed a bill of particulars. As a description of power relations in general, two referred to the "Byzantine" style of administration (*C5; B6*) that historically has impressed its mark on Russia, leading to a "very closed form of politics ... intrigue ... perfidy and submissiveness" (*B6*). Along these lines, one respondent argued that the influence of political clans is inversely proportional to the measure of democracy in the country – a

---

[5] There was a single exception to this pattern in the corpus of interviews given by former members of El'tsin's administrations. One respondent from that group claimed that "Russian politics has always been Byzantine ... The El'tsin period, of course, was distinguished by Byzantine politics. Then, personal contacts played an enormous role and El'tsin himself was a master at this art of establishing personal contacts" (*C5*).

measure that he estimated as near nil (*A2*) – while another likened its rules to

> some kind of mafia groups united to preserve their power. They have no political principles. None. They are not united by political ideas, only by the idea of defending and consolidating their own position … The requirements of society are, practically speaking, not taken into consideration. These days there is only a sharing out of property, a sharing out of power. Look what is transpiring in the government of Moscow with the mayor's office. They're clearing the field for someone there, driving out the entire coterie of [Yurii] Luzhkov [the mayor – M. U.] which had run things there. The same is true in Nizhnii Novgorod and Kaliningrad. This is called a "lateral movement". It means in the first instance that now the influential, powerful people will be their [Putin's] people. In the second it means that these people will execute decisions taken behind closed doors. You could call what we have in power now a "Masonic lodge" (*D3*).

These comments on the success of the Putin clan in subduing its regional rivals contrast with another respondent's illustration of personalized relations within Russia's government. In reply to a conjecture that recalcitrant officials might mend their ways if the prospect of dismissal from their posts hung over their heads, he argued that

> laws and the chain-of-command do not work here. Officials know this and their partners all know it, too. If an official is fired, then the system of personal acquaintances and trust relations that he has in the bureaucracy is destroyed. And his replacement won't be able to administer anything until he cultivates for himself these same ties … I have never encountered a situation when they removed a notable *chinovnik* [a disparaging word for a state official – M. U.], or he retires, and the ministry or some powerful division of the Administration of the President literally didn't

disintegrate. Everything had been held together by him personally and until you restore that situation, nothing will work.

Take the city of Krasnodar. A big part of their budget goes to cover their debts from previous years. All that is done in the city now is financed by a deficit. And the task of the mayor and his people is to convince people to work, guaranteeing them through personal ties that the debt to them will be paid out of future revenues. This is all accomplished through agreements. But if the official in question were removed, then the agreements would be destroyed and misfortune and tension would occur. In a word, big complications. Everything is done on the basis of personal trust, someone's personal obligations to someone else ... I can be absolutely precise. In the municipal sphere, as the Soviet system worked, so things work today (*C*4).[6]

The conflicting surfaces of these narratives – one describing a federally based clan imposing its will on their counterparts at municipal level; the other showing how officials at one or another station are insulated from directives coming from the top – should not conceal the fact that they both converge on the central point: *viz.*, respondents regard not institutions but personal networks as the grid through which power flows.

Teams. Respondents generally assigned a far more favorable evaluation to their work in teams. Whereas "clans" were usually associated both with others and with wrongdoing, "teams" evoked a principled collaboration yielding the good. This may be occasioned by the fact that teams do not involve extended networks with roots in

---

[6] The political sociologist Ol'ga Kryshtanovskaya has offered a comparable assessment of the importance of personal ties in the Russian state bearing on the issue of bribery. In response to a journalist's question concerning the motivations behind the legislature's 2008 passage of an "anti-corruption law," sponsored by the Kremlin, along with a simultaneous year-long suspension of its implementation, she remarked that the legislature "perceives corruption as a stabilizing factor! In other words, corruption means everything's normal, that's how things work – you can pay some extra money and whatever you want gets done ... But if punishment follows, it would lead to disorganization" (quoted in Samarina, 2008).

the economy but are more or less task-specific groups. Typical of the recitation of that experience would be the remarks of two respondents from the first El'tsin administration.

- My colleagues in the department worked conscientiously. It seemed to me that they wanted to do what I wanted to do. Together, we experienced joy in this as well as some misfortunes ... When people are given the opportunity to do good, positive things – even if they were not taught earlier to do this – then they experience a sort of emotional satisfaction. That satisfaction helped me to work, as did the presence of a certain number of like-minded people (B2).
- The first moment in my political career was joining the Leningrad–Moscow group of [Egor] Gaidar and [Anatolii] Chubais, which created the preconditions for entering politics and the first government of Russia in 1991 ... We had not been part of the system and, in a way, this helped, especially those of us who had come from Petersburg. The Moscow establishment had zero influence on us ... Because no one knew us, no one came to ask favors. This is very suitable [udobno] as a matter of fact. It lowers the influence of lobbies enormously. This also relates to the present period in which many, many people have come with Putin from Petersburg. They are very much protected from the influence of Moscow interests (B6).

These remarks represent the basic elements of the "team": some general goals toward which the group is oriented; a common outlook on matters related to the team's performance; a collective experience of the results of their efforts; mutual, as well as personal, satisfaction in achieving group goals; and some insulation from the influence of clans that reinforced team boundaries.

However, not all comments on the team form of organization were necessarily positive. One respondent noted how the cloistered conditions under which his team functioned produced "an aberration of consciousness," a condition that he traced to the

> influence of the institution on your brain, perverting your notion about what is going on. Even if you try to avoid this, it goes on

anyway. It's inevitable ... [Even when I was in office] when the mass
media were free, you would read newspapers, watch television,
converse with journalists and this would go on all the same. Because
journalists would not look on you as a person with whom it is
possible simply to communicate, but as power with which to do
something or other. Your position begins to pervert your brains (C6).

In another instance, a respondent similarly remarked on a team of
economic reformers that he had joined long after it had begun to
function collectively.

I hadn't been a member of the economics *kruzhok* [a group of
like-minded people working on a particular subject – M. U.]. I didn't
need any *kruzhok* to learn what capitalism is. [I had lived in the
USA] and that was part of my everyday work about which I had
written. But when the reforms were undertaken, then the
experience within the *kruzhok* was more important than the
experience of actual, living people ... Therefore, the reforms were a
little bit idealistic from the point of view of capitalism. My favorite
joke – thought up by East Germans – was that what Marx said
about socialism was nonsense, but what he said about capitalism
was true ... It was excessively naïve of those in the *kruzhok* to
accept this. But this was connected with their inadequate education
and with the fact that they formed a tight-knit clan close to the
leadership. These were objective factors blocking the success of
policy (B1).

In the case of one group of respondents working in the Administration
of the President, members commented at some length on the conditions of work that cemented their team identity and action. The
frequency of their interaction appeared as a central factor, "practically
living together around the clock" (C1). Echoing the remarks of others
on the team (C3, C5), one member described his situation this way:

Here's my work day. I get up in the morning at a state dacha. I get
into a car and go to work where I sit until 10:00 in the evening.

> I converse only with my own people. At 10:00 or 10:30, I get into a
> car and go to the dacha. I sleep. On Saturdays I also go to work.
> Sunday is a day off. I sleep. Later, I go out and stroll the grounds
> of the dacha. I meet [Evgenii] Yasin, or someone else among the
> well-acquainted people who are from the same circle. All the time
> one's contacts are the same (C6).

All members of the team reported being united by a common idea, but
that idea – "reform" – was sufficiently vague to allow for differing
interpretations in concrete instances. Thus, consensus was produced
out of "long arguments, long disagreements" followed by "people
consciously withholding their opinions after a certain point in the
discussion and acceding to those who had more expertise in the
area" (C1). Thus, on all but one occasion, unanimity eventually
prevailed (C3).

However, unity within the team was also promoted by personal
relations cultivated in various ways, and it would appear that these
rivalled, if not surpassed in certain instances, the force of a common
idea, especially when that idea formed the basis of the "long
arguments, long disagreements" themselves. Among the means
mentioned for promoting group cohesion were birthday parties and
the breaking of bread. With respect to the first of these – an important
ritual in Russian culture – one respondent remarked that:

> when birthdays occurred we would all get together and
> congratulate the person having the birthday ... You could say that
> in many respects we were like brothers and sisters, like relatives ...
> We knew each other very well, we understood each other, we could
> sense each other's feelings (C1).

Another remembered that:

> we had a ritual of gathering every year on El'tsin's birthday,
> without El'tsin. We would get together for a couple of hours, have
> some vodka and champagne. At first this occurred because of
> El'tsin's invitation, and then in other years when an invitation

wouldn't come we just took it upon ourselves to get together in a restaurant. We would commemorate his birthday and praise one another [saying] things such as "there has never been such a team and in the future there will not be," and so on. Out of this experience, I can say that we were not just a team of intellectuals but we became very close friends (C3).

El'tsin's role in maintaining group unity appears to have been paramount, and is discussed momentarily, below. Here, notable would be the importance of his symbolic presence at the birthday gatherings despite his actual absence from the table.

Tables constituted the hub of the team's integrating rituals in other ways. On certain occasions members would gather to enact some of the ceremonies related to the production of comradery, not unlike the goings-on at birthday parties for an absent El'tsin, in which the ostensible purpose of the gathering was overshadowed by the process of generating group affect and solidarity. Regularly, the team would gather at a government installation on Lenin [now Sparrows'] Hills to stage a send-off for presidential representatives heading out to assume their duties in one or another province.

We had a large dinner at this place [on the first such occasion] and everybody really liked it. So we decided that we will gather like this after every new presidential representative had been dispatched. There we would assess how well things were going, what we could do better ... It was a very warm situation. I don't know how many times I was there but this ritual was steadily observed. We looked forward to this moment, not so much the designation of the envoy but the aftermath ... We were able to get together and congratulate and praise one another (C3).

On a more quotidian basis, a bout of tea-drinking before each workday provided another fraternal atmosphere for personal interchange, sometimes work-related, sometimes not. These occasions were organized by the female member of the team, described by another member as "in some respects, the heart of our team" (C3). She remembered these occasions thusly:

> Every day I would receive the entire team in my office. There was a very large, beautiful table there that came from the office of Aleksei Kosygin who, you remember, worked for a very long time as head of the government in Soviet days – a much respected individual. Every morning we would drink tea there and I would bring in snacks to go with the tea and coffee. Various things, some that I myself had picked up while I was on vacation. And during this time of tea-drinking we would discuss the various tasks that we expected to accomplish that day. We would share information, the problems we were having and so forth. And behind this table there seemed to be such good fellowship ... It was our tradition every morning to have a chat, to joke around a little and get ourselves ready for the day. These 30–40 minutes of tea-drinking were invaluable. Since I was the only woman, I had a special right to criticize and even to badger the men. But this would have to be accomplished in a very soft or indirect way (C1).

In addition to the import of personal relations reflected in these comments, gender seemed to have played a particular role in the maintenance of group solidarity. On the female side, the woman occupied a particular position of nurturing, both materially with the provision of comestibles, and non-materially with "soft" criticism. The respondent in question also alluded to the overall eufunctional effect supplied by "the softening factor" of feminine participation, warning, however, that the team "doesn't need a lot of women because then the group would probably break up into couples and you really don't need that. But in this context you have to have women. Just one or two" (C1).

Through her eyes the role of the male gender also falls into sharp relief, especially the figure of "papa," represented in this case by El'tsin. With respect to relations with others outside the team,

El'tsin would play the role of protector, insulating the team from external pressure.

> The group was able to work peacefully during a period of constant crisis because the president screened off the group from this crisis, screened it off. Because people from the ministries would come to us, important people from the ministries, representatives from the leadership of the Duma, representatives from the Supreme Court. They would come and tell us about the things that they didn't like in our work, or in El'tsin's speech, or in policy plans. They would criticize what we were doing. El'tsin would intervene and say to us, "I understand how many people are coming and complaining to you, but I am not going to hand you over to them" (C1).

On the side of intra-group relations, El'tsin's paternal role seemed of equal importance.

> El'tsin would regulate relations among members of the group. He would listen to their complaints, he would hear their expressions of dissatisfaction and he would correct them. "No, no, no," he would say, "that's not your worry. That's his [or] that's hers. That's not your concern, it's mine." It was very much like a kindergarten in that respect. There is a *vospitatel'* [teacher or master] and then there is a group of children. In a given case, this *vospitatel'* has to regulate the group. And the *vospitatel'* is able to do this if he has the wisdom and understanding. And if he doesn't, then the group is regulating itself which means, practically speaking, conflicts and collisions within the group … El'tsin showed himself to be both very delicate and very experienced in this regard (C1).

Taken collectively, these comments from members of the team that had served in the Administration of the President under El'tsin illustrate the highly personalized character of social relations in Civil Society *II*, transposed in this instance onto the structure of their formal roles in government. They register a high level of affect within the group that not only pervades their work environment but spills over into occasions away from the workplace where team identity and solidarity are rehearsed. Strong ties within the group produce and, in turn, are reinforced by representations of the other with whom they interact, representations that accentuate some threat posed by the other to the team and its members.

The conceptualization of threat and protection against it summon up a familial discourse, an amplified version of social relations based on strong ties. The collection of images and related roles within it provides a template for relations among group members, contributing a certain logic or rationale to their interaction. Thus, El'tsin is cast in the role of "papa," holding at bay unwelcome intrusions by outsiders and, as *vospitatel'*, sorting out squabbles – real or potential – among group members. The male members of the team, accordingly, appear as sons and brothers. They evince close, affective bonds manifest at various celebratory sites that also are apparent in everyday work settings, whether at the regular morning tea-drinking session, or in a small smoking room where non-smokers would bum cigarettes from other team members in order to partake in this bonding ritual (*C3*). The female member – "in some respects the heart of our team" – takes on the character of "mama." She not only adopts a nurturing posture toward the sons/brothers but "softly" points out their shortcomings, bringing them along (if not "up") in the proper way. She warns against the ruinous potential that more female members would represent, not only disturbing her role as "mama," but posing a sexual threat to team solidarity, which would translate into the familial discourse as incest.

CONCLUSION

The epigram at the head of this chapter appears to be a half-truth. Viewed through the prism of Civil Society *I*, it may well describe interpersonal relations in post-communist Russia. However, when the lenses of Civil Society *II* are put on, things look quite differently. Trust among those acting within its informal structures – conceptualized here as power networks, whether of the clan or team variety – seems to be in copious supply. It is reflected in the comments of respondents – whether describing the behaviors of others or recounting their own experience – as a high level of affect for which a familial discourse is employed. In the case of the other, "clan" is the pivotal category; for one's own team, relations are rendered along the lines of the nuclear family and its gendered roles. The half-truth in the epigram, then, applies to the other. Where strong ties predominate, trust accorded the other would exist in inverse proportion to that experienced within the group.

The representations of the political world offered by respondents appear to conform in all respects to the elements in the Civil Society *II* model. Inasmuch as the abstract categories of the model correspond to the actual experience of respondents, the model has a certain claim to validity. But it remains a model, nonetheless. Its utility consists in its ability to provide a shorthand for social relations in a Russia no longer state socialist, yet one that by no means has been transformed into a version of capitalist democracy as implicitly posited by the model of Civil Society *I*. The import of the Civil Society *II* model thus might be found in this recognition of difference and in the concomitant inference that the social relations characteristic of contemporary Russia are neither an empty space – because they do not resemble those specified by Civil Society *I* – nor a deviation from the way that things (somehow) should be. Rather, the sinews of the social find explanation in the forms of capital that underlie them. When the embodied forms of cultural and social capital predominate, then social relations express this embodiment in personalized fashion, just as respondents express themselves in these same terms.

The modal patterns of organization on Russia's political landscape – "clans" and "teams" – thus inform the habiti of participants. Their knowledge of background practices in this world tells them whom to trust, whom to avoid, what can be expected from confederates or outsiders, where protection might be found. These reflections in consciousness of the social relations in which actors are embedded structure their political discourse, thereby allowing for inter-subjective intelligibility, no matter whether parties to communication are involved in concord or disputation. If the model of Civil Society *I* can be construed as congruent with the ideal type of political discourse outlined in the previous chapter – thus enabling statements about "Who?" (competence), "What?" (morality), "For whom?" (community) and "How?" (approval) – then the very different ensemble of social relations associated with Civil Society *II* would conduce to a very different discursive structure, one in which the elements of community and approval have been eclipsed by the particularistic loyalties, identities and processes of recognition summoned up by the terms "clans" and "teams." The following chapters explore that discourse rooted in the relations comprising Civil Society *II*, beginning with its shrunken sense of community.

3   Community

There has always been the problem of alienation of the
state from the population. People don't regard themselves
as the source of power, although they go to the polls,
they vote. But inside themselves they draw the line
very finely. (C2)

This chapter focuses on the language of community, on the ways in
which Russian political actors join together signifiers related to state
and society in order to construct community as a discursive object.
As such, the purpose here is to extend the discussion of social
relations in the preceding chapter into the area of social ontology,
exploring how the words of respondents produce a conception of
community congruent with those social relations themselves. The
word "ontology" refers to that which appears in the eyes of the actors
as something that is "there," something that is not their doing but
something with which they must somehow reckon. Narratives about
community are like that, portraying social relations in objectified or
"frozen" form (Cassirer, 1944, 1946; Lefebrve, 1969). Because the
community which the speaker invokes can be separated in language
from that same speaker – who talks about "it" – a discourse of
community involves an act of alienation, not unlike Karl Marx's
([1867] 1906) "fetishism of commodities", Georg Lukacs's "reifica-
tion" ([1919] 1971) or Benedict Anderson's (1983) "imagined communities." In all three instances, words give life to a construct
apparently existing unto itself. As this chapter shows, the discourse
of community articulated by Russia's political class both constructs
such a community and undermines that very construction. Traces
of existing social relations in their narratives continually subvert the
thing-like character of state and society and sustain an image of
community fractured by antagonistic, personalized relations.

STATE

Language about the state commonly portrays it as a thing. Why? Is not the state a part of us, our (not infrequently involuntarily) doing? Despite the fact that the state is fashioned by human hand, however, it appears in social consciousness as an entity standing apart from society, as some agent that surveys, assesses, enumerates and enjoins society from its presumed vantage of the whole (Scott, 1998). This thing-like character of the state is, of course, something that must be produced, and states – or, better, those who run them – have, indeed, devised numerous and obviously effective ways to produce it (Bourdieu, 1999). As Timothy Mitchell (1999: 77) has put it, the "phenomenon we call 'the state' arises from techniques that enable mundane material practices to take on the appearance of an abstract, nonmaterial form." This transformation can be likened to the one depicted by Michel Foucault (1977) in his study of "disciplines," according to which all manner of human activity in modern societies has been subsumed by abstract codes specifying the precise ways in which given activities are to be performed. Just as Foucault's disciplines lead two lives – they both inform human activity and simultaneously stand outside of it as measuring rods and guides to action – so Mitchell (1999: 89) observes a comparable process in the action of the state. In its institutions

> the precise specification of space and function ... the coordination of these functions into hierarchical arrangements, the organization of supervision and surveillance, the marking out of time into schedules and programs, all contribute to constructing a world that appears to consist not of a complex of social practices but of a binary order: on the one hand individuals and their activities, on the other an inert "structure" that somehow stands apart from the individuals, precedes them, and contains and gives a framework to their lives. Indeed the very notion of an institution, as an abstract framework separate from the particular practices it enframes, can be seen as a product of these techniques.

Thus, Mitchell's "state effect" refers to power's work on social consciousness, engendering the apprehension of the state as a freestanding, autonomous entity – a thing – rather than a particular terrain on which the process of producing and deploying social power is carried on.

As the interview narratives disclose, the "state effect" is rather weak in contemporary Russia. When personalized power networks, as discussed in the preceding chapter, dominate the landscape of government and politics, institutions do not display the impartiality, rationality and attachment to established procedures on which that effect is predicated. The dynamics of state formation and disintegration in the post-communist world – in which power centers in the economy and society have been able to advance their purposes not by pursuing strategies that strengthen a rule of law protecting their private interests but by invading the domain of the state, seizing the assets that socialism had stored there (Ganev, 2007; Reddaway and Glinski, 2001; Hedlund, 1999; Solnick, 1998) – may well explain this pattern. Despite this relative weakness, however, the Russian state remains a presence: arbitrary, lawless, corrupt, extortionist, unpredictable – but a presence all the same.

For a number of respondents, the state seemed to personify a faceless bureaucracy that presented itself as an impediment to their actions. One from the Gorbachev-era cohort recalled how the centralized state apparatus, choked with torpor and indifference, hindered his efforts at provincial level:

> Half the taxes collected in our region were assigned to the region
> itself, the other half went into the federal budget. Do what
> you want with that money. You want to build a sauna … you
> want to – but you couldn't. You'd have to travel to Moscow and get
> permission for anything … So I began to build things simply in
> hooligan fashion. It was necessary to get permission, but I'd say,
> "We don't need any. Start building and that's it." That's how things
> got built. If we were waiting around for permission, then we'd still
> be waiting around till now, and we still wouldn't have it (A4).

Another from the Putin-era cohort remarked that:

> Bureaucratic narrow-mindedness always interferes. Our
> organizations are very much afraid that someone will do
> something. They don't like to cooperate. They like to do
> everything themselves. And therefore many things are done
> wrongly (E1).

Those from the El'tsin era mentioned much the same:

- Policymakers attempted to solve problems, as it were, substantively
  and bureaucrats would put up formal obstacles. Sure, there were
  procedures, but as a matter of fact they could be used, so to speak,
  by the bureaucrats in their own interests (B6).
- I am heading the research institute [in my organization]. We have
  worked out a method for evaluating laws that detect their potential for
  corruption. A scientific method. You can put it into the computer, load
  in a projected law, and its capacity to generate corruption [becomes]
  evident. We are prepared to render expertise on all laws with respect
  to this theme. But they [bureaucrats] don't much want this. We have
  given [them our] expertise along these lines for the water code, the
  forest code and for the law on advertising. The bureaucracy doesn't
  like us (B10).
- After the Vienna Conference [on human rights] in 1993, we, much
  inspired, returned and decided to compose a program for the
  development of human rights in the country. We worked for about
  three months. Here you have my department [in the Ministry of
  Foreign Affairs] where I'm already up to my neck in work, and we
  nonetheless prepared a very fine document, outlining which concrete
  steps must be taken to improve the human rights situation in the
  country. Even El'tsin approved it in principle, not to mention [Andrei]
  Kozyrev [then foreign minister – M. U.]. But according to formal
  procedures, it then had to go through all of the ministries for their
  approval. And at this stage all was lost. Because the ministries
  understood that this was an additional headache for them, interfering
  with their normal life, their functioning, and so they deleted every

proposal, which, in fact, amounted to the entire thing. So this document never went forward (B2).

- On November 6 [1991, Leonid] Kravchuk – then president of Ukraine, which had just voted to secede from the USSR, and it was clear then that the entire country [USSR] would collapse both politically and economically – arrived [in Moscow]. According to the recollections of eyewitnesses, someone from El'tsin's circle rang El'tsin, saying: "Boris Nikolaevich, you have already pronounced a reform program, but nothing is going on. We don't even have a government." During the break between negotiations and drinking [with Kravchuk], El'tsin signed the first decree on our appointment. That's how we were appointed. But, of course, the *apparat* [bureaucratic officials – M. U.] was extremely against this. They thrice "lost" the decree on my appointment and then spent more time rewriting it. In the document, the word "minister" appeared with a small "m" but a capital "m" was needed, or vice versa (B9).

In the same way that a sclerotic federal bureaucracy has posed problems both for those at the center and for others in the provinces, so provincial bureaucracies are claimed by one respondent to be the source of the same malady.

> [In the early El'tsin period] officialdom was then transparent
> [*otkryto*], political competition at the federal level was still strong,
> and El'tsin wanted in no case to destroy it, inasmuch as at the time
> it was neither intense nor rough-and-tumble. But at the very
> moment there was a funny, strange situation in the regions where
> harsh authoritarian regimes were established, and political leaders
> controlled the political opposition, the press, the economy,
> information – what have you – while at federal level there was
> powerful, intensive political competition. In this sense, that's what
> we have now, simply the transfer of regional traditions to the
> federal level. Nothing more . . . Because Piter [St. Petersburg – M. U.]
> has not been "capital number two"; it is too much a provincial
> center. Now this provincial mind-set has come here and, naturally,

has begun to establish a situation convenient for itself out of its basic notions of what's permitted and what's not (*C6*).

The common thread running through these apparently divergent comments on the geographic location of the problem seems to be access to the means of administration for which personalized relations serve as "a little magic key" (*B8*). In the absence of this key, respondents report on state organizations as closed, indifferent and subversive of both order and direction because the keys in a given instance are held by networks to which they do not belong. This condition produces a dual consciousness. From a distance, respondents perceive the state as a bureaucratic phalanx, as illustrated by one who recited a passage from one of Leon Trotsky's writings:

> "The attempts of the White Russian émigrés to overthrow Stalin make me laugh. Stalin has surrounded himself with a tight-knit stratum of the party and state bureaucracy which is satisfied with its position and will not permit this to happen. A few decades along, this bureaucracy will want to have its own privileges independent of the will of the Central Committee of the Party. Privatization will begin. Then the time will arrive for a real proletarian revolution" (*A2*).

However, when observing things closer to hand, the visage of the state shifts abruptly to a tangle of fractured elements, plotting, maneuvering and warring with one another. One respondent described his experience in the foreign service thusly:

> Any ministry, any department, including the Ministry of Foreign Affairs, the KGB, the Central Committee of the CPSU ... was similar to a layer cake. There was a layer of liberals, a layer of democrats, and it was always necessary to undergird our bureaucratic games [intrigues – M. U.] so that the right person [was contacted] and brought in on the matter, so that the issue did not leave our liberal circle. Because if the matter fell into other hands, you could considerate it dead (*A1*).

He then went on to demonstrate the process through which action would transpire in officialdom by means of a story concerning the USSR's decision to foreswear the use of psychiatry for punitive purposes, a process initiated, incongruously, by his team in the Ministry of Foreign Affairs.

> The Central Committee had issued a memorandum on the necessity of adopting a new law on psychiatry ... We needed to obtain a few signatures on it, one of which was that of the Minister of Health, Evgenii Chazov, who was then considered to be a big liberal, a big democrat. But Chazov was a furious opponent of psychiatric reform and the liquidation of punitive psychiatry. For me this was completely unexpected ... So we [in the Foreign Ministry] initiated a visit to the USSR by a team of American psychiatrists led by the internationally known Loren H. Roth. We had exhausted all of our internal resources of struggle and had achieved very little. We had managed to free a lot of people from psychiatric hospitals and to get some half-measures from the Prezidium of the Supreme Soviet, but this was very, very little compared with what had to be done. So we used the levers of pressure against those categorically opposed to psychiatric reform. We thought up the plan to invite the Americans who couldn't not support unequivocally our own recommendations. We fully knew the mechanisms operating within the country and abroad. And thanks to the Americans' visit, the law was passed (A1).

This story of bureaucratic intrigue and the avoidance of established procedures had a happy ending: punitive psychiatry was abolished. Respondents told other stories that had similar outcomes. One recalled how, as deputy prime minister in 1993, he would fly around the country with suitcases full of rubles in order to pay the wages of miners and other working people because officially appropriated funds had a habit of disappearing in the process of their transmission to the regions, and seeing to it that these workers were paid was critical to maintaining a modicum of support for the government (B10). Another, recounting his experiences in the Ministry of Foreign Affairs, described how the Russian delegation to the Geneva Commission on Human Rights refused to follow explicit instructions from their ministerial superiors, insisting that all participants in the Commission must criticize *their own country's* human rights record before pointing the finger of blame at others. Initially considered as "idiots" by those from other delegations, the Russians eventually made some progress in introducing these unorthodox methods into the world of international diplomacy (*B2*).[1]

But unhappy endings were mentioned, too. On the tragedy enacted at a Moscow theater in 2002 where Chechen terrorists took hundreds of hostages during a production of the musical "Nord-Ost" (some 200 of whom eventually perished due to the authorities' use of gas and their exceptionally dilatory behavior in getting initial survivors to hospital), one respondent remarked that:

> [the authorities] had set up headquarters there [during the siege by Russian forces] in order to save the hostages. I sat there the whole time. Other deputies [of the Duma] came and went. The situation there was more or less under control [*normal'no*], but there were a lot of people. Then these paramilitary forces who were directing operations brought in a bus where they sat by themselves and permitted no one to enter, only those whom they needed. Some of the people who were in that bus told me that the soldiers were having a full-scale booze-up, with vodka bottles standing right there on tables. That's the way that things are here, even during such a tense situation (*D4*).

---

[1] This same respondent also discussed the matter of Russian policy at the Commission, where the delegation negotiated with their respective ministry on how Russia's position on human rights during the First Chechen War would be presented. The outcome was a twofold compromise. "First, we would have the right to express our own personal point of view [condemning Russia's human rights violations]. Second, we would try to support the state position as much as possible, but only to the degree that it didn't contradict our views and our relationship to what was going on in Chechnya. They accepted this" (*B2*).

These episodes illustrate the double character of the state in the ontology of political actors. On one hand, it constitutes a presence that sometimes can be circumvented, sometimes not. It might be faceless but by no means is it inanimate. On the other, the "state effect" is weak. Discursively, an explanation can be provided by the analysis of legal discourses constructing the modern corporation offered by A. J. Greimas (1990b) who notes that in this instance a board of directors – whom he calls the "legislative assembly" – not only establish the function of management, but also deprive management of the power to act on the corporation itself. Discursively, then, management and the company become one and the same thing, owing to the fact that management cannot distinguish itself from the company by acting on it. By extension to the political sphere, the executive becomes the state, commissioned (in principle) by others – voters, legislators, constitutions – to act on the outside world but denied the right to act on itself. In the remarks of respondents, however, an altogether different situation prevails in Russia. The executive continually acts on itself.

> When the president is elected he doesn't get power but the right to struggle for power which he must do for all four years. The same is true of the legislature. Elections are only a ticket to the struggle for power ... El'tsin always struggled for power, and after 1993 [the year of his putsch – M. U.] perhaps even more furiously. When I worked in the Administration of the President, I took part in this. El'tsin struggled for power with his own government. Our economic administration was created as an instrument to help El'tsin against his own government (*C*4).

Greimas's "legislative assembly," which can confer the state effect by denying the executive the right to act on itself, represents the role of law in political discourse. Its relative absence in Russia is recorded in the narratives of numerous respondents who concurred with the notion that it is members of the executive that have denied the Duma the right to act at all. Among the many respondents who commented on this, here are two of the more poignant examples:

- A machine now works there. Two-thirds of the votes belong to United Russia [the main Kremlin party – M. U.] and there's no opposition. "Where, who?" – no one knows their names. There is an element of the herd in this. Everything is decided in the faction [of United Russia]. Moneyed interests now understand that they don't have to pay money to get candidates elected, they pay the ones who have been elected (B10).

- The Duma is a big voting machine. When we were in it, there were these secretive lobbyists whom practically no one ever saw. For example, there was [a certain] Dubov, a deputy [of United Russia] who never spoke on the floor, on television, nowhere. That would have been counterproductive for him. He worked only to shell out money [bribes – M. U.] to the deputies so that certain bills would be passed. The deputies would go to his office and sell their vote cards to him, even those from United Russia, and he would distribute the cards to those who would vote "correctly" – to his own people – arranging them like sentries at the moment of voting. Once when the vice-chair of the budget committee was reporting on a certain bill, this Dubov was talking on his telephone and suddenly approached him at the podium: "Well, let's have a little talk" (D4).

SOCIETY

The French Revolution's seminal accomplishment was to usher in the era of modern politics and government. Its principal achievement in this respect was to inaugurate "the people" as the central category around which all else would revolve (Furet, 1981; Hunt, 1984; Sewell, 1994). In part, "the people" is defined by a putative commitment to the commonweal that necessarily takes umbrage at the privileges of the rich and powerful. By casting out this other, an imagined "we" is produced (Laclau, 2005) that is the sponsor of Habermas's "communicative power" referenced, above. Some two centuries after the watershed of the French Revolution, "the people" reappeared on the stage of Russian politics (Urban, 1990; Sergeyev and Biryukov, 1993). But not for long. Whereas political actors of all stripes were quick to invoke their name during the country's anti-communist revolution, that practice began to die out in the 1990s. As the interview narratives recorded for this study indicate, references to "the people" in the language of Russia's political class have become both infrequent and not uncommonly execrative. Above all, "the people" are assigned no agency. In the best light, they appear as supplicants: either immediately and with their conscious participation; or from a distance, as receivers of supposed benefactions of which they are themselves unaware or toward which they may even be negatively disposed. The narratives of respondents who did direct remarks to "the people" can be subdivided into four general orientations: the people as inert; as in need; as degraded; as manipulable. This section explores each in turn.

The people as inert. Referring to Russia's cultural traditions, one respondent quoted the philosopher and publicist, Igor' Klyamkin, who wrote that:

> "among our elite there exist two opinions about the Russian people [*narod*]. On one hand, there is the people as god-bearers, very spiritual and with high ideals. The other variant is the people as vegetables who understand nothing, not even goo-goo." And another of our philosophers set the prompt that "these are perfectly commensurate: vegetables/god-bearers. For one reason or another, they understand nothing about politics and their political opinion can be ignored. That is, they don't understand because they are vegetables, idiots, and because they are god-bearers"[2] (*C5*).

---

[2] I have used the plural in this translation of the respondent's remarks in order to render them in common English usage. In the Russian, however, the singular appears consistently. The people [*narod*] is likened to a god-bearer and to a vegetable which "understands nothing" and so forth. This linguistic aspect of Russian thus constructs a single entity – the people with its own agency, even if that agency appears as lack of understanding, irresponsibility, torpor and so on. For an elaboration on the category of "the people" in Russian cultural practices, see Ries (1997).

Although this respondent disclaimed any truck with this conception, seeing it as a conceit of the "Moscow intelligentsia," his remarks as the interview progressed seemed to place himself on the side of adherents to the vegetable/god bearer thesis. Addressing the matter of elections and emphasizing the importance of understanding the electorate in order to make effective appeals to them, he characterized the typical Russian voter as "largely unable to sort out politics. He is subject to various phobias, some kind of irrational influences, which are very difficult to manage. He is unpredictable and it's very difficult to foretell his conduct."

Alone in the sample was one respondent who took a different view of popular involvement in politics.

> Nowadays, anyone says whatever he wants to, on television or anywhere else. There is no point of view that is inaccessible. But [during *perestroika*] it was altogether different. People only said what they really thought to close friends, only in the confines of a smoke on the stairs or in the kitchen. [Therefore] when I spoke at public meetings there was such a silence that you could hear a fly buzzing under the ceiling ... I said simple things. El'tsin had already been destroyed, not for advocating a multi-party system but for saying that such a thing should be considered. And when I went on television saying that we needed a multi-party system, all Moscow responded. On the following day, I simply couldn't ride the bus; all the passengers were ready to take me in their arms and carry me ... And when the proceedings of the first Congress of People's Deputies [May, 1989 – M. U.] were broadcast, you could hear only one thing on the street: the Congress ... In the shops, the sales person would be listening as she wrapped up your sausages. The customers in line would be listening, too. On buses, in the metro – everyone had a radio on. But that was then. Now, everyone lives a "normal life" thinking about where to save a ruble and where to make one. Fate is no longer afoot. The Berlin Wall can only be torn down once (B5).

Even in these positive comments about political involvement, popular participation appears as both passive and transitory. Things, in the end, seem to return to their normal state. Those particularly active during *perestroika*, as was the interlocutor just quoted, report that subsequently there have been "no public political forces in society, no real political force" (D3). Rather, what appears is "Russian psychology, a huge deficit of political culture and, the main thing, a deficit of political culture among the elite" (A5).

Along these lines, two respondents commented with considerable indignation about the view of the electorate taken by certain political actors:

- A week ago, I was at the headquarters of the Union of Right Forces and this really hit me. They don't have any confidence in the voters, they are not even attempting to win them over. And these are the liberals! (C5).
- There is a group that completely believes in its right to rule the country ... I know that [Vladislav] Surkov [deputy head of the Administration of the President – M. U.], when he speaks before the cadres of United Russia, uses the term "biomass" to refer to the population (D4).

These views are further elaborated by a story related by one respondent about his experience on the barricades thrown up in defense of the Russian government during the August putsch of 1991.

> I have a plot of land in the country. I had a neighbor there,
> a peasant. He was also on the barricades, and during all that
> craziness there, he wrote a petition to El'tsin requesting his own
> plot of land. And he brought it to El'tsin there, and El'tsin signed
> it with "yes, I agree." Afterwards, when my neighbor got home, he
> went to the local authorities and they actually gave him a big piece
> of land. Then they gave him a tractor, a house, geese, a cow and
> whatnot. Within ten years he had drunk up all of it. And now again
> he has nothing (E1).

The people in need of help. In a few instances, respondents remarked on efforts to use their positions to assist constituents. Without supplying details, one said that he saw his calling in politics as rising to the defense of those impoverished and betrayed by the economic reforms of the 1990s (E3). Another, who has a considerable history of direct action, street-level politics – as well as an impressive record as a legislator – avowed that his efforts were all bent toward "attempting to help the maximum number of people" (D4). A third respondent went into considerable detail about the casework that she had performed as a legislator at both municipal and national levels. A short excursus on her narrative sheds light on a path present on the terrain of Russian politics, albeit one rarely traveled.

For present purposes, perhaps the most important thing to know about this individual has already been disclosed by the use of the feminine pronoun "she." Much like the other woman in the sample, discussed in the preceding chapter in the context of a "team" working within the Administration of the President, the highly gendered role that she enacted could be described as "nurturing." In this case, however, the nurturing was directed not at work mates but at citizens who came to her to complain about a long-standing grievance in Soviet/Russian politics: housing. More than issues of physical comfort are involved here. Because the state has established waiting lists regulated by explicit procedures, for many questions of justice are every bit as much a part of the matter as is the apartment to which they are entitled, but which has been usurped by someone with pull.

This respondent (D5) described herself as someone alienated by the usual patterns of government, whether those of state-sponsored youth organizations in the Soviet era – "in the fifth grade I began to understand that all of that was false" – or, later, by executive structures in municipal and national governments that she was invited to join but eventually left because she was "too honest to work there." Moreover, she was the only person in the present survey to have interpreted the question about establishing "good personal relations with people" as pertaining to constituents rather than to others in the political class. Here is how she described her experience working as a deputy on the Moscow City Council and, briefly, in one of its territorial divisions in the housing office.

> I couldn't relate to the [other] deputies/odd-balls on the Council, who held reception hours for their constituents once a week. Once a week! During most of my time on the Council, I conducted open receptions – that is, till I just couldn't see any more people. True, the number visiting me became so large that receptions would go on till ten o'clock in the evening and I still hadn't seen them all. It was impossible. Working in the housing office, I got piles of letters and appeals from citizens which I would take home and compare to the legislation in effect. I also wrote up the disposition of these matters for the housing office, adding my own conclusions. This led the *chinovniki* to dislike me immensely. But thanks to this work, I became well known in the city with 25 percent of Muscovites able to recognize my name. This meant that my election campaigns got maximum results with a minimum of financing. Simply because people knew me. Grandmothers, grandfathers, aunts, uncles, young people would take my flyers, clutch them to their breasts and take the campaign from door to door ... I'll say it again, I am not a "meeting" [public gathering for speech making – M. U.] deputy. I can't tolerate those speeches from the podium, except for the ones directed to actual matters, those which explain and clarify our rights, especially in the housing sphere.

This respondent's remarks are exceptional for other reasons, too. Their concrete tonality and insistence on addressing the expressed needs of constituents sharply contrast with the more remote dedication to popular welfare evinced by others in the survey. To a certain extent, all respondents seem to have spoken from a subtext reading: "I am in public service not for self-aggrandizement but to serve the public." However, "public service" would usually mean, in context, something like designing programs or writing laws that will benefit society. When more specifics were requested during interviews, the replies ran in the direction of programs not enacted,[3] or those that had been but with undesired outcomes.

> The date 21 August [the defeat of the 1991 putsch – M. U.] I think should be a national holiday. The victory of the revolution opened up the possibility for reforms to solve the country's burdensome problems ... But by autumn 1996, our period of romantic revolution had ended ... The sources of opposition [to the reforms] and to those people who were able to understand them lay with the fact that they destroyed the basic worlds of people, having affected their root, living interests, and this couldn't be avoided. Therefore, all of this should be considered, when people's wages are reduced to the point that they are insufficient for existence, enterprises are closed and so forth (C7).

The people as degraded. The most extreme version of the people-as-vegetables thesis appeared in the narrative of one respondent who argued at length that Russian society has been degraded. In strange symmetry with the remarks of *C7*, just quoted, he contended that rather than a curtailment of reforms due to an uncomprehending (but suffering) population, the reforms themselves were to blame for not only impoverishing the population materially but for introducing an unbridled capitalism that has corroded mass culture. In this rendition, then, the people are not "vegetables" by nature. Rather, their victimization at the hands of an unscrupulous elite explains their degraded condition. This respondent's (D2) metaphor of the shepherd and his flock – quoted in the preceding chapter – represents the subtextual hub of his narrative.

---

[3] For example, one respondent (D7) on this prompt referred me to a book of reforms put out by his party (Yavlinskii, *et al.*, 1995).

In 1989–1991, it was not a good thing to be on the take. If a responsible official was practicing deception, that was bad. Now it's normal ... And the most burdensome result of this, above all, has been the degradation of society, the introduction into our society of vulgar-liberal notions, liberalism as the unlimited freedom to enrich oneself. This model makes it easy to place other people under your control. A significant part of our elite has been totally bought off. They seek their dignity and solicit praise not in their own country but abroad. That's where they send their children to live and to be educated. That is, we have adopted the African pattern: our elite associate themselves not with their own country but with gaining entrance into the world community.

The general atmosphere in our country has become that of the vulgar market. You can see television shows portraying heroes who ... well, the day before yesterday I was watching a show called "Striptease" where the girls were saying, "Yes, I think that my work takes great fortitude, it requires self-control and the ability to take yourself in hand." They spoke as though they were talking about pilots, cosmonauts or prominent surgeons. But they were talking about striptease!

Take our monument to Pushkin over there. If you look at it from the side, you won't see Pushkin any more but the casino, Shangri-la. You'll see a huge billboard for Neva beer, but not Pushkin. That's degradation. I can't imagine that anywhere around the Lincoln Memorial in Washington you'd see a big billboard for anything, not to mention something for beer or a casino. In my view, our situation stems from a direct contradiction between the interests of business and those of society. Business, selling us commodities, needs a slow-witted, trusting consumer into whom it is easy to hammer the idea that he urgently needs some commodity and must buy it now.

The people as manipulable. Although no one else in the sample went into such detail or expressed the same combination of revulsion and regret at the current condition of Russian society as did *D2*, some of the remarks already cited – say, those referring to the electorate as "phobic" and "irrational," or the derogatory appellation of "biomass" – indicate a certain receptivity in the political class to his idea of degradation. Others concur with his observation that the consumer-voter is easily manipulable. One took up this idea from the point of view of populism in politics, which in the Russian vernacular is a term of opprobrium.

> El'tsin was a populist genius. He was super ... [In politics] there is
> either populism or integrity, probity and sincerity. Two contrary
> things. But the success of one or the other depends on the
> development of society, whether society is prepared to notice
> integrity in a certain politician and vote for him, or whether
> society is glad to be deceived, to be for the populist who shakes
> his fist and orates.
>
> Gorbachev tried to show integrity and probity. Gorbachev
> tried. And what happened? No Gorbachev. El'tsin was a super
> populist. The result? He tore down the country and handed it over
> to the devil's mother with his "shock therapy," throwing it into
> penury (*A4*).

Finally, another respondent reached the same conclusion as did the two preceding ones concerning the deplorable state of Russian society, but he arrived at it from an altogether different direction. Rather than the vulgarization attributed to unbridled capitalism or the readiness of average Russians to be duped by nefarious politicians, he located the root of the problem in the particular geopolitical and cultural situation prevailing in the country.

> Given our present levels of human resources and growing
> technological lag, we will no longer be a great power [*derzhavoi*].
> We will be a very strange territory on which a competition between
> the new and old poles of civilization will unfold. This is dangerous.
> But these ideas are absolutely unpopular. Sometimes I attempt to

speak about them on television. I understand that for the majority
of people they stir up resentment and rejection. [That is why] just
from the point of view of our national interest it is necessary to
slowly but surely surmount the authoritarian syndrome that exists
in mass consciousness. This will take a generation of the right kind
of education and much, much, more (C6).

CONCLUSION

Under the rubric "ontology" has been placed, here, those forms of
community apprehended by respondents as simply "there." This
cognitive orientation represents a social practice that organizes perceptions according to certain categories, constructing thereby
"things" standing apart from the subjects unmindful of the fact that
these "things" are in the final analysis the orchestrated, routinized
forms of their own social practice. These "things" structure cognition, they comprise a part of habitus, they enter into those conscious
or unconscious calculations informing action (Bourdieu, 1977, 1984,
1990, 2005). They can be anticipated, used, avoided, manipulated and
so forth, but, from the vantage of their *existence*, no one can do
anything about them.

Organizing the remarks of respondents according to two broad
categories – state and society – this chapter has found splits in the
ontology of Russia's political class. With respect to the state, their
comments disclose an entity that, on one hand, appears faceless and
immutable. It seems to stand as a brick wall of bureaucracy impeding
their plans and actions. Members of each sub-sample attribute this
character to the state – a phalanx of officialdom who might be outwit-
ted or out-maneuvered in a given instance but which nonetheless is
there tomorrow as that same brick wall. On the other hand, however,
an image emerges from their comments that is at loggerheads with
that apprehension. In this second instance, it appears that the bricks
themselves have agency. They are not simply obstacles to action,
mired in routine and inertia, but plotting, maneuvering, warring

elements on the terrain of government and politics; they appear as power networks pursuing their own agendas from within the apparatuses of the executive. Both of these images of the state seem consistent with the relations specific to Civil Society *II*: the "brick wall" of impenetrable officialdom represents the personal appropriation of public office and its correlate, the absence of a rule of law; the idea of bricks with their agency indexes the role of informal networks in that same context.

The resolution of these conflicting images might be found at the level of practice, conditioned by proximity. That is, when action is at close range, one's competitors or opponents become apparent. The subject knows that if a certain initiative should fall into their hands, all might be lost. In these instances, the subject thus organizes his world according to the model of power networks. However, when the other is more remote, when names are not known, there seems a greater likelihood that the subject's cognition will employ a shorthand for the state as the brick wall of bureaucracy.

With respect to society, there appears to be a near-complete consensus in the respondents' remarks that the citizenry seems unable to comprehend the political world, and is thus politically inert and incapable of mounting any action. However, contrary images appear in the comments of two respondents. One references a short span of time in which the population, albeit rather passively, was involved with political life, showing acute interest in the affairs of state during the late *perestroika* period. The other points to intense and sustained popular involvement in her electoral campaigns, owing to her reputation as a legislator prepared to act on their expressed problems in the matter of housing rights. Her narrative stands out from all others in this regard, joining popular demands to an agency that responds to them and eliciting, in turn, a popular response to the maintenance of that agency. Hers appears to be a full-fledged political discourse and represents the lone example of such in the sample.

Among the other respondents, however, images of the people as inert, degraded and manipulable dominate their narratives.[4] How does one in public life go about serving the interest of *that* public? The answer given by respondents is generally to prepare comprehensive programs – which the public will neither understand nor appreciate – that will (allegedly) better the condition of the uncomprehending. This discursive construction of "the people" in Russian politics – vegetables and/or saints – is congruent with the cultural notion of *sobornost'*, a concept connoting a mystical communion of the population in which all particular and venal interests have been superseded by a common spirit, a common understanding and the general will. Previous analyses of speeches on the floors of the Soviet and Russian legislatures have disclosed its structuring presence in debates where it serves as a supercession of practical matters that propels communication onto the plane of the purely mythic (Sergeyev and Biryukov, 1993; Biryukov and Sergeyev, 1993; Biryukov, Gleisner and Sergeyev, 1995; Gleisner, Byzov, Biryukov and Sergeyev, 1996). Subjects thus cast themselves in the role of relays for this supposed general will, positioning themselves as worthy by virtue of their articulation of it. In correspondence with this agential power arrogated to themselves by speakers, the category "the people" undergoes a commensurate diminution of capacity. The discourse of *sobornost'* is by no means the only one employed by Russia's political class, but it does constitute a recognizable presence on the political field. "In Russia," in the words of one respondent, "you have *sobornost'* as a form of democracy" (*E3*).

The existence of the opposing images of state and society recorded in the interview narratives is consistent with the model of political discourse employed in this study, which posits the possibility for interaction among its elements in the course of actual speech. Here, the narratives of respondents do not conform to a

---

[4] As Stephen White has shown in a recent study based on focus groups composed of rank-and-file citizens, a comparable, but morally inverted, discourse prevails among "the people" themselves. His subjects report that they are generally ignored by those in power, except at election time when sham forms of participation are made available to them (White, 2005).

particular discursive practice; in the case of both state and society, they display quite different ways of thinking about these "things." For example, "community" usually appears as a weak construct, composed of individuals who are ignorant, manipulable and so on. In one version, that community is hitched to a discourse of competence enabling the speaker, or others to whom he or she gestures, to overcome the shortcomings of the population by taking compensatory measures on their behalf. In another, that same community is conjoined to a discourse of morality, according to which the population's degraded state is explained as a product of the measures taken by nefarious rulers. In itself, this situation is anything but startling, inasmuch as this sort of reversibility in discursive play – that is attributing the existence of some condition to diametrically opposed factors – is not uncommon on the field of politics anywhere (Edelman, 1988; Lakoff, 1996). Here, my purpose has been no more than to investigate the Russian variant of these discursive practices in order to determine the specifics of how those in that country's political class construct their cognitive worlds.

4 Morality

> You're a member of a tribe, and among your own
> there's one morality, while for those who do not
> belong to the clan there is another (C6).

This chapter concerns the moral dimension of Russian political discourse. One of the prompts given to interview subjects directly mentions "the role of moral principles in politics," but their discussions of moral issues were by no means limited to responding to it alone. Rather, the fact that many of them included moral considerations in their remarks on a number of other topics indicates the salience of this factor generally in the discourse of Russia's political class. I wish to underscore the point that my consideration of the topic, morality, has nothing to do with codes of conduct pertaining to individuals, themselves, much less to whether they abide by them in practice.[1] Rather, the focus falls on moral *discourse*, conceptions of the good circulating in the political class on which individuals can draw in order to locate themselves in the world of politics, to express their identities and justify their actions, and to characterize the behavior of others. As the remarks of the respondents make clear, moral discourse often intersects with themes of competence, community and approval.

The chapter begins by juxtaposing two discourses organized around the idea of securing the good or the right while constraining the arbitrary use of political power: discourses of law (approval) and morality. It then moves to an examination of morality exclusively inasmuch as narratives rooted in legal discourse were both infrequent

---

[1] For a study that examines practical morality in contemporary Russia, see Lundh (2008).

and abbreviated. In this respect, it discovers that, for Russia's political class, morality is not all of a piece. Indeed, very different, even opposing, versions of morality prevail among its members. In conclusion, an interpretation and explanation are ventured in order to account for the different discursive patterns evident in the interview texts.

LAW AND MORALITY

In general terms, the interview narratives identified two means of obtaining the public good while restricting arbitrary political activity: one would presuppose the existence of a formal, institutional order articulated in legal relations; the other references some established moral code. Against each of these was opposed an informal, personalized world often characterized as a Hobbesian free-for-all wherein power networks represented actual political relations while legal or moral structures were, at most, something to be manipulated or circumvented. One respondent, whose remarks would represent, *sotto voce*, views expressed by many others regarding the influence of law and morality in politics, contrasted contemporary Russia with "stable societies that already function according to external principles inserted into their matrices such that the standard rules of conduct play a big role. Therefore, in such places, personal relations may not be so important [as here in Russia] inasmuch as there is some standard of conduct which you are obliged to observe" (*E2*).

Law, as such a standard of conduct, has not enjoyed a particularly commendable reputation in Russian history and culture. Viewing the matter through the prism of the national literature, Yurii Lotman (1992) has noted that the category, law, connotes a dry and impersonal basis for human relations that exists in sharp contrast to human qualities such as love and compassion. Thus, *law* appears not as an extension of *morality* but as something actually opposed to it. Consistent with that binary structure, the notion of *politics* is negatively conjoined to *piety*. Within the cultural system described by Lotman, then, both law and politics have historically occupied the space of the alien or the negative, opposed to – rather than coincident with – society's conception of the good. Along these lines, an ethnographic study of Muscovites conducted in the 1990s discloses a comparable tendency to consign all politics and politicians to the category "dirty." In so doing, subjects are able to construct identities that have both a moral content and a sense of personal agency, inasmuch as abstaining from the false world of politics represents part of a choice about dealing with the many practical matters associated with survival (Shevchenko, 2008). These observations on the positions occupied by politics and morality in Russian history and culture are generally borne out by the interview narratives reported here.

Taking firstly the matter of law, a number of respondents directly referred to its irrelevance in Russian government and politics. Here is a sample of their comments:

- Our work in the Auditing Chamber showed that in our country civilized institutions for controlling power can work, and work effectively, but for building the [entire] state, one, two or three well-placed bricks are insufficient. If all the remaining elements of the legal system – procuracy, courts – don't work, then the information that we produced just disappeared and wasn't demanded by society (D2).
- I won't name the minister who in his day staggered me by the fact that not only had he not read a law governing his sphere of authority but he didn't even know that it existed. And when he learned of it, he still had no desire to read it and to find out what had been written there ... For the minister, his legal position was altogether unimportant for his work. For him, the system of personal contacts was enormously more important (C4).
- We have a state apparatus. If today the law were strictly applied to these *chinovniki*, then surely every second one would come in for either criminal or administrative punishment (E5).
- Corruption is born in the normative acts [laws – M. U.] themselves – imprecise rules, the arbitrary power of the *chinovniki* [coded as] "at your discretion" (B10).

The only positive comments about law in Russia registered in the interviews came from three individuals involved with the legislative process. One mentioned a very effective law on the mass media passed by the old Supreme Soviet (C4); another recounted a number of socially important laws passed by the Duma in which he had a major hand but noted that most of them were either weakened or cancelled by subsequent legislation (D4); a third also referred to his authorship of beneficial legislation but noted how the terms of these laws were often radically reinterpreted in their implementation (E 2). Given the negligible importance assigned to law by those in the sample for establishing a standard of social and political conduct, the discussion now turns to morality as a culturally more resonant route to restraining arbitrary and rapacious political power.

MORALISTS

The perceived importance of morality in the affairs of government and politics was articulated by one member of the sample thusly:

> Amorality, which ascended the throne in our society after 1991, is one of the basic and most difficult of our problems. The second is absolute disrespect for law. But amorality is even more [important] because morality is seminal; it is fundamental in Russia. In Russia, where the law has never mattered much, we nonetheless have attempted to live according to moral principles. But the basic problem in particular of the reform decade [the 1990s – M. U.] has been a militant, celebratory and licensed amorality (A3).

Morality, then, is regarded as a force that might compensate for the weakness or absence of law. But the problem does not end there. The culture's reception of morality also seems to admit to a binary formulation. In the words of another respondent:

> In Russian politics, we have very strange traditions: there is this strange mixture of extreme idealism and extreme cynicism. In the first place, a real politician must be a grand leader [vozhdem]; he must forget about himself and think about others. But on the other

hand [you'll hear] "And what are they doing?! They have all sold themselves out a long time ago. They're all scumbags [*svolochi*]." This is completely absurd, and thus it seems to me that there is a lesson here (*C5*).

As if elaborating on this double-sense of morality in politics – "extreme idealism and extreme cynicism" – another respondent said the following:

> A working commission was convened by the Supreme Soviet and members of El'tsin's government to overcome legislative resistance to the proposed plan for privatization. The Agrarian Party until then had militantly opposed the government's plan. [Anatolii] Chubais [representing the government – M. U.] said to the agrarians: "You have wanted us to write something in here for you?" They had in mind the privatization of the rural reprocessing industry. "We'll write that in for you." After this, the agrarians got up and left. And the majority of them who had been backing the Supreme Soviet's position switched sides and joined the government's position on all the other measures in the plan. I was terribly mortified and I swore at them: "How immoral! We must stick together. You got your bit only because we have all stuck together. You got yours, then you just toss off everyone else" . . . They have this peasant trait. Immoral? Difficult to say. I then understood how they understand their own interests . . . If you encounter such a thing which you internally perceive as moral, it means that you simply understand poorly why one or another person does what he does. It was you who didn't think it through, who didn't understand. That is, you are the more guilty if you have such problems (*C4*).

Perhaps the key phrases in these remarks are "such a thing which you internally understand as moral" – a marker for idealism – and "you simply understand poorly why one or another person does what he does" – an acknowledgment of the other's cynicism and a caution to expect just that in the world.

Those in the present sample seemed overwhelmingly to associate political activity with cynicism and immoral behavior. Indeed, that negative evaluation of politics might explain why twelve of the thirty-four individuals in the sample – among them, government ministers (including a prime minister and a deputy prime minister), a deputy leader of a political party, deputies in the national legislature, and directors of policymaking organs in the Administration of the President – in one way or another *denied* that they had had political careers. Moreover, four other respondents, who did not eschew identification with past or present political activity, claimed either to have been coaxed into it by others or, in one case, to have entered the political arena because of the death of his mother, a trauma that he linked to the consequences of the economic reform of the early 1990s that propelled him into politics in order to protect the weak.

A characteristic shared by nine individuals denying that they had political careers, and by two of those claiming to have been dragooned by others into one, consists in the fact that they had already established academic careers before involving themselves in government and politics. However, fourteen others in the sample with comparable backgrounds did not reject the notion that they have/had been politically active, thus indicating that those denying such involvement were signaling more than the fact that they had entered politics through the passageway of the academy. Rather, they explicitly argued that political activity was something that they had shunned because it was dirty, depraved or morally repugnant. To one extent or another, nearly all individuals acknowledged the accuracy of that assessment. In the words of one respondent:

> At bottom, people who go into politics do not do so to achieve some national or worldwide goals, but do so because they can acquire power over other people. Even worse, some do it just to utilize that power to make money . . . They go into politics just to use power for large-scale theft. [For instance, those from Yukos] paid not only deputies of the State Duma, not only members of the

Council of the Federation, not only governors, but members of the government and members of the Administration of the President. And they managed to gain access even to the FSB ... This is terrible. For the sake of enrichment, to privatize the state? (D1).

In those of another:

As the elite formed [in the mid-1990s], new criteria [for political success] emerged – it became especially important to have the support of politico-financial groups. A politician had to have dirty hands, had to steal and so forth so that his boss could keep a personal file on him in his safe. That way, he would be obedient ... All notable posts must be occupied by people on whom – like in the days of [J. E.] Hoover – there is a dossier (B10).

Statements such as these underscoring the venal aspects of politics represent a semantic reversal that might be read as: "I am calling attention to this because things *should not be* this way. Politics *should* be moral." That reversal seems to be part and parcel of the moral discourse articulated, above, by the respondent referring to the dichotomy of "extreme idealism" and "extreme cynicism." Indeed, both extremes appear in some of the interview narratives, instantiated by one respondent who claimed during the interview that the lesson that he has drawn from his experience "is always one and the same. There are a lot of rogues, scoundrels and cynics in politics, people who seek power for power's sake." However, as the discussion progressed, his comments turned to the other side of the dichotomy, noting that:

The lessons of the 1990s [show] the possibility for contemporary Russia to become the active cultivator of a new humanism for the twenty-first century. Our country and nation have always been associated with heroic accomplishments, with the capacity for exceptional compassion and mercy. But they laugh at us for this, because we are disorderly and don't know how to husband our own resources. In Europe, there's even a joke: "Russians are strange.

It's simpler for them to devise an all-terrain vehicle than to repair their roads." Well, I don't want to devise a planetary all-terrain vehicle but realize that the life of each concrete person and his specific problems today in my native Russia [are reflected] in the fate of humanity on a planetary scale requiring that same measure of wisdom for their solution (B4).

The co-presence of these extremes locates our speakers within a broader consensus on the essential importance of morality to political life. In the texts of their interviews, it continually recurs as an equivalent to the folkloric sought-for-thing. Although this perspective is certainly not unique to Russian political subjects, the frequency and intensity with which this concern has been voiced by those in the present sample would appear to set them apart from their counterparts in politics where law plays a larger role and, thus, where political struggles are more manageable and regarded as part of the normal routine. The relative novelty of public politics in Russia finds its cognitive complement in an inexperienced political class disposed to substitute moral categories for political ones.[2] This substitution reflects a cognitive strategy whereby the unfamiliar and unfathomable are rendered intelligible by translating phenomena relevant to one sphere of endeavors into the terms characteristic of another. In so doing, the subject analogizes while remaining unaware of the fact that he or she is employing an analogy. What seems novel about the Russian case is not that a moral discourse substitutes for a political one. Rather, it consists in the fact that whereas mass publics – without direct knowledge of the political process and with small attention to it – readily make this substitution (Lakoff, 1996), whereas in the present instance this substitution is effected by members of the country's political class itself. Thus, the denial of having had a political career appears as a stark example of constructing politics by means

---

[2] A second discursive substitution involves the replacement of politics by professionalism, the topic of the following chapter.

of a moral discourse, a discourse that expels politics as morally reprehensible behavior not bearing upon the self but upon *others* who engage in it.

From a cognitive vantage, the implications of this substitution of a moral discourse for a political one are critical. It invites *misrecognition* in the sense first outlined by Pierre Bourdieu, who regards its socially significant version as collective, systematic and constitutive of effectively all relations of power in human affairs (Bourdieu, 1977, 1984, 1990). That is, innumerable social transactions – and especially those involving exploitation and domination – depend for their success on at least one party failing to ascertain the significance and import of the transaction itself. Alena Ledeneva has effectively employed Bourdieu's concept in her study of *blat* relations in the Soviet Union, showing how *blat* – the illicit appropriation of public resources – had required the misrecognition of the parties involved in it. *Blat* would transpire through chains of personal relations in which reciprocity was generalized, rather than specific to particular individuals. In this scenario, individual A would approach B complaining of some lack that he or she could not fill. B could not fill it either, but B might then go to C who had an acquaintance D who would have access to the resources needed. D would then pass along the required items or considerations through the *blat* chain until they reached their specified destination, A. Although *blat* was stigmatized culturally as a theft of public property, none of the parties to this reticulated exchange would regard it as stealing. All were performing favors to aid a soul in need. Yet, the stigma remained culturally relevant and, accordingly, the perception of others in comparable *blat* transactions elicited moral censure. Consequently, as an institution based on misrecognition, *blat* appeared to each as something that others did, others who would be execrated as greedy and unscrupulous people. But as far as oneself and one's circle were concerned, these same relations were consecrated as assistance to those in need, a form of help that conditions, the shortage economy, required them to perform in order to demonstrate their moral character (Ledeneva, 1998).

It appears that a comparable process of misrecognition informs the relation between politics and morality for many of the respondents in this study. Here, not so much individual blind spots but culturally sanctioned modes of expression are critical. That is, all respondents have access to the discursive code labeling politics as an activity that should represent a moral undertaking, but all around there is evidence in practice to the contrary. In the face of this incongruity, moral considerations offer an explanation – politics has been highjacked by immoral forces – that enables subjects to distinguish themselves from immoral others, going so far as to deny in some instances that they had participated in politics at all. Within this discourse of morality, the issue of political corruption neither engenders an analysis of this phenomenon on its own terms nor inspires practical measures aimed at altering those conditions or systemic features occasioning corrupt behavior. Rather, as in the *blat* syndrome, blame becomes the central category. Corruption simply references bad people doing bad things. Here are some examples of how this discourse was articulated by respondents:

- I have come to the view that the kind of person you have tells you the kind of politics he engages in. If he is shit (excuse the expression), then that's the kind of politics he has (*A*4).
- In Russia now it is very fashionable to talk about, more precisely, to laugh [at the idea of] morals in politics, at morality in politics. It's very fashionable to say that politics is a cynical business (*A*1).
- Who has been successful in Russian politics? People who are able to lay out views that are broadly disseminated, those which people easily recognize. People who have no moral principles and who therefore might change their point of view at any moment, might easily be liable to corruption, who easily go in for theft and privatization, for murder (*D*1).
- [In Russia] there are two or three definitions of "success" in politics. The first and most broadly applicable, I would say, concerns the quotidian: he who doesn't murder, hasn't sat in prison and hasn't grown rich. Second, he who has survived, hasn't sat in prison and has

remained an active politician with some influence. And third, he who has remained his own person, has not grown rich and has not become a politician – that's me (*B1*).

As is particularly evident in this last set of remarks, the immoral other frames the moral self. The reverse moment, affixing moral probity directly to the self, occurred less frequently among respondents. Here are some remarks typifying it:

- Moral principles for me play a colossal role. Therefore, I am not now [involved] in politics ... For a political career [morality] is a brake, some kind of limitation. But without moral requirements, a person, particularly in politics, moves in incomprehensible directions. That kind of politics cannot last long (*A2*).
- Morality holds the principal significance, the key. That's all. It is more important than all the rest. It can't be sacrificed. Otherwise, everything else is senseless (*D6*).
- I have not striven to be engaged in politics. I have not striven to participate in under-the-rug games. I haven't wanted to buy or sell anything, to be involved with trade (I have in mind the trade of mutual concessions). Of course, I understand that without compromises, generally, no sort of social life is possible. But compromises mustn't take the form of trade (*B3*).
- I think that politics can and must be done with clean hands. This does not exclude making compromises ... but compromises must have their limits, and these one must never transgress. Politicians are often amoral, but amorality occurs among critics, scholars, surgeons and engineers [too]. It's not an exclusive quality of politicians. Therefore, I think that morality in politics is an absolutely necessary thing (*D7*).

Aside from indexing one's moral stature, these comments are disrupted in the final two sets of remarks by an acknowledgment of practicality in politics, the need to compromise. But this acknowledgment is immediately negated by an insistence that compromise – as far as the respondents are concerned – must be strictly confined to that which, from their point of view, is itself moral.

A variation on this view – one that magnified the intensity of moral claims – involved self-sacrifice. Sometimes the scale of this self-sacrifice appeared comparatively modest, as in the case of one respondent who pointed out that, as a deputy in the Duma serving his second term, he was offered an apartment which he refused. "This was due purely to moral principles," he maintained, arguing that "I didn't have the right to take for myself that which at that time was one of the basic problems of my voters – the housing problem" (D3). However, in two other cases, the stakes were considerably higher. One legislator described a death threat delivered in his presence to the governor of Magadan, a threat made good shortly thereafter and one that by implication included the respondent himself (D2). Another legislator described her work verifying the legality of the allotment of housing in a central district of Moscow:

> I found a mass of violations. And somehow about two or three weeks after this, on my return from my first meeting with my constituents, a car ran into us on Tverskaya Street. It was a head-on collision and I ended up in hospital. They were afraid that they would have to remove my liver, but, glory to God, that didn't happen. But here I've got two fingers that still don't work. And the driver who crashed into us was hidden away from the scene. Up to the present day I don't believe that this was an accident (D5).

A few other respondents raised the theme of political martyrdom, sacrificing their careers in politics for the sake of moral principles. In response to a question about his main accomplishments in politics, one incongruously listed his resignation from Boris El'tsin's cabinet, due to his perception that the reform program that he had authored and that had been formally adopted remained a "Potemkin village." Further on, he spoke of how his opposition to the Second

Chechen War seemed to cost him some two-thirds of his constituency going into the legislative elections of 1999, and how:

> Most of my own party criticized me [for this]. The best of them agreed with [my stand] but said that I should say it in other terms. But how do you say it in other terms? In other terms? There are no other terms here! I think that I said it inarticulately. It was necessary to say it even more harshly (D6).

One of his fellow party members commenting on that same decision noted that:

> I thought that he should have acted otherwise. This cost us a lot of votes. But he was acting more in correspondence with his own internal feelings than with real politics. Unconditionally, this was politically damaging. But because of it we are now able to be the idols among the human rights community. But that's a very small group in society (D4).

Another respondent recounted with pride how he had left his political party while serving in the legislature due to principled differences over proposed legislation, an episode that followed the even more gratifying experience of catching out crooks in regional governments, for which he himself was soon sacked (D2). A fourth respondent claimed that he was "too honest to work in the [executive] structure" and accordingly left (D5), while a fifth refused a ministerial post in the Russian government in order to maintain his party's principled opposition to it – a decision that he says he has lived to regret (D3). A sixth expressed his admiration for Sergei Stepashin for resigning as Minister of the Interior after Chechen fighters' successful raid on Budennovsk in 1995, and for an earlier resignation from another high state office in 1992 when his draft of a new constitution was rejected, a decision in which the respondent joined him at the time (B10). Finally, one member of this group, refusing political office because of moral considerations, referenced a distant other in order to frame the venality of the proximate ones with whom he could not associate himself.

Russian political culture doesn't love gradualness, it doesn't love reflection. It loves ready-made solutions, harsh evaluations and so on. This – and here's the point – is the root deficiency of Russian political culture, in the framework of which there is no feeling of conscience whatsoever.

Like a fool I used to think that moral values played some role in Russia. I was very proud that I was opposed to the collapse of the USSR, against the shelling of the White House [location of the old legislature – M. U.] and had refused many ministerial postings offered by El'tsin, because I considered him to be an amoral person. But such things don't upset anyone in this world. There are some politicians who present themselves as patriot-statesmen. They had been with [Egor] Gaidar, with El'tsin and then they switched over to [Gennadii] Zyuganov [Communist leader – M. U.]. None of this bothers anyone! Perhaps in the West morals play a larger role. I know that [Angela] Merkel sold out [Helmut] Kohl on her way to becoming leader ... But on the other hand, she is decent. Recently, I was in Berlin and they showed me her home and the shops she goes to. Right there! And no one is assassinating her (A5).

PRAGMATISTS

A counter-code also surfaces in the interview narratives, one that relativizes moral imperatives and excuses moral lapses on the basis of unfavorable circumstances not of one's choosing. This is the discourse of know-how, one which Ledeneva has recorded in a more recent study as central to state and business practices in post-Soviet Russia (Ledeneva, 2006). Here, know-how represents, above all, knowledge of how to break the rules in order to accomplish one's ends. In this study, it has appeared in the interview narratives under terms such as "political professionalism," a designation usually carrying a negative moral valence. As with Ledeneva's respondents, those in the present sample employing the counter-code demoting the importance of morality would plead their own cases by availing themselves of the moral escape hatch of necessity. They would blame others for the conditions in which they have been forced to operate and point to others who do even worse. This counter-code is in fact a variation on the culturally dominant notion that politics should be a moral enterprise. In either case, the possibility that self- interest is a driving motivation is concealed, either behind moral categories or by disclaimers about the impossibility of abiding by them. These codings, in turn, recall the discourse of *sobornost'*, indicating that Russian culture makes small room for the political moment in the country's political discourse; *viz.*, the recognition of difference and the acceptance of the inevitability of conflict. It would seem that "self" remains a culturally suspect notion in Russia and that outward manifestations of its negation or sublimation continue to correlate with the professed code of conduct (Kharkhordin, 2000; Lotman, 1990). This condition may be a moment in the larger scope of transitions from communism, in which a lexicon suitable to articulating the self within new and unfamiliar circumstances has been largely unavailable to social actors (Verdery, 1996, 2003; Ries, 1997; Humphrey, 2004). Presented with that for which cultural categories make no allowance – in this case, the acceptability of selfishness –social actors may reassert with even greater insistence categories to which they are accustomed (Bourdieu, 1977).

In contrast to those underscoring the import of moral-political principles, others emphasized pragmatism as a consideration motivating their decisions to enter and remain in political office, despite their moral misgivings. One respondent claimed that he wished to resign his post in the executive when the First Chechen War was launched but was dissuaded by Aleksandr Yakovlev – Gorbachev's architect of *glasnost'* and thus a voice of moral authority – who argued that his replacement would only make things worse (*C6*). Another placed his own principles in the context of political loyalty and realism, noting how he had argued in the national press against the passage of a certain law involving clearly political principles but eventually voted for it due to the importance of maintaining party discipline. "I have developed a formula," he maintained, "that distinguishes our party from many others: 'preserve and multiply'. . .", he continued.

To do this:

> One must lean on the old ... on the experience of the Soviet
> Union and a thousand years of Russia. On our traditions such as
> communalism, mutual aid and collectivism ... Even if one wanted
> to transplant the Protestant ethic to our soil, it wouldn't work ...
> Our tradition is that the state is mama and papa. That's good or
> bad: but it's our tradition! [All this is necessary to take into
> account] in politics where the main thing is [getting] results (E5).

One of his colleagues echoed these remarks, but with a certain
darkness of tone.

> A great deal in politics today resembles the film *Ty mne – ya tebe*
> [Roughly: *You Scratch My Back, I'll Scratch Yours* – M. U.] ... And
> there are two negative sides to this. First, it becomes very difficult
> to refuse when they ask you to do something. Your flexibility level
> in these relations becomes higher. Second, in relations with a
> number of people, you are unable to evaluate them objectively.
> I therefore solve this problem for myself rather simply: No matter
> how you ask, I will never criticize a group of acting politicians;
> I won't give negative evaluations of their conduct even in that case,
> when it seems to me that they have done extremely negative
> things. But, glory to God, these people don't do such things (E2).

The persuasiveness of these arguments is not nearly as important for
present purposes as is the fact that the arguments are made. That is,
those who reference episodes in which their moral integrity might be
called into question are themselves able to access the moral discourse
from which it arises, even as they shunt their narratives onto another
track.

VERSIONS OF POLITICAL MORALITY

Turning to the matter of morality in politics in a more direct sense –
that is, putting the question: What is it that can make politics a
moral endeavor? – our respondents were split into two groups. One

referenced loyalty and trustworthiness in interpersonal relations, while the other tied their notion of morality to faithfulness to abstract principles. This distinction was not lost on some of the respondents themselves, one of whom claimed that:

> A clan morality functions today, [one involving] faithfulness to one's clan, a moral order within the clan, like in primitive societies. You're a member of a tribe, and among your own there's one morality while with those who do not belong to the clan there is another ... Concerning abstract humanitarian values, the Ten Commandments, well, I think that today this isn't working. Moreover, it would look strange in these times, it would conflict with loyalty. Not to steal budget funds when your group is in position to do so would signify disloyalty ... Present-day politics is cynical. I have the feeling that there is even pride taken in this. A part of this is that even a term [for it] has been thought up: "He's a good 'professional'" (C6).

Taking these versions of morality as poles, our respondents can be placed along a continuum bounded at one end by group loyalty and at the other by devotion to abstract principles. Starting from the latter pole, a cluster of respondents explicitly disavowed any truck with compromise or pragmatism when it came to moral issues (D1, D2, D6, D7). Although some in the sample also spoke about the need for compromise in politics, each embraced the view – noted, above – that compromise could never concern one's moral principles themselves (D2, D4, D6, D7). In words that would capture the sentiments of most, if not all, in this group, one respondent offered the opinion that "we would not have had the privatization that we did [i.e., both grossly unjust and economically ineffective – M. U.] if we hadn't believed that we cannot get to the 'radiant market future' [parodying communism's perennial – and now, laughably discredited – promise of such a 'radiant future' justifying today's sacrifices – M. U.] over the corpses of others. [Anatolii] Chubais [privatization's chief superintendent – M. U.] would be an example of this cynicism.

'Let them all die [he might say], 'we'll build our radiant future on their bones'" (D5). Notable, here, would be the implication that the absence of moral controls – reaching the "radiant market future" over the corpses of others – unleashes the forces of darkness and ruin. Inasmuch as this discourse of morality references only inner rectitude as a means to restrain these dark forces, it appears to isolate itself from political practice. Indeed, it exemplifies that dichotomy, quoted above, wherein moral absolutism is housed under the same roof as moral cynicism. Exponents of this discourse underscore their participation in the former by consigning their political opponents to the latter.

Interestingly, everyone in this study who spoke in terms of moral absolutism belongs to the sub-sample, "democratic opposition." At one time or another, they have all been members of Yabloko, whose principal competitor and initial *raison d'être* was provided by the other major group in Russian political society claiming the name "democrats," namely, those associated with the economic reform wing of the first El'tsin administration (White, 2006; Urban, 1994a). Because they have shared a common language, liberalism, disputes between these two groups have been especially intense, reminiscent of sectarian feuds, as the above remarks on privatization and the "radiant future" would suggest. As if mindful of the moral arguments deployed against them by their democratic opponents, two of those responsible for the economic reforms resorted to a sort of hyperbolic pragmatism in order to justify their past actions. One version concerned the timeliness and importance of the reforms themselves.

> I think that the greatest achievement of our government was not even the fact that it laid the basis of a market economy; rather it consisted in the fact that it rescued the country from famine and freezing during the winter of 1991–1992. The main thing was that it rescued a country with nuclear weapons from [a situation in which] the nuclear button could turn up in the hands of madmen (B9).

Another involved the constitutional crisis of 1993 and the violent termination of the country's legislature, immediate reasons for the formation of Yabloko.

> The crisis had to be solved by adopting a new constitution, some specific constitution, any constitution, but one that worked. This was clear to Boris Nikolaevich [El'tsin] and to myself, working then in the government. We already knew how a crisis of dual sovereignty [*dvoevlastiya*] ended in a bloody mess [i.e., the Bolshevik Revolution – M. U.]. A nuclear country could not have lived long under the situation that existed then (*B8*).

Both sets of comments quoted, above, trump moral arguments by raising, and then vanquishing, the spectre of nuclear holocaust. Again, their persuasiveness is not at issue. Rather, it is the fact that both arguments suggest a sensitivity to moral criticisms that respondents seem to be unable to answer on straightforwardly moral grounds. Hence, the shift not only from morality, but from economics and politics, to a discourse of survival.

Moving by degrees toward extreme cynicism – which, naturally, is always ascribed to the other by respondents, and never used to characterize the self – a number of those in the sample also spoke of achieving some golden mean between principles and pragmatics (*A1, A2, A3, A4, B4, C4, D4, E1*). One respondent placed these terms in dialectical opposition, noting how an absence of pragmatism in actual politics emasculated one's moral principles in the practical order (*C2*). Another from the Putin-era cohort noted that:

> In politics, the main thing is results. Results. If you don't know how to get results, you are a poor politician. Then why are you in politics? You have to know how to listen to your own partners, to your party comrades, to your opponent. In my view, you must find the right compromises. That's the highest acrobatics in politics, [doing this while] preserving your own principled position (*E5*).

Similarly, another from this group remarked that:

You can be guided by this principle: absolute honesty in politics can be considered as absolute stupidity. And simultaneously it would also be incorrect to say that in politics you are dishonest, because always in politics you must choose for yourself those qualities unavoidably necessary to yourself. I have tried to think about this because you often encounter those calls to take decisions which make you feel uncomfortable. And maybe from the standpoint of idealism it would be simpler to get up and say "You can all go to the devil." And leave and toss it all aside. But evidently flexibility – which is present in me – won't permit me to do this ... As a result there are a great many people who evaluate my conduct in politics as immoral. And there is an equal number of people regarding it as moral (*E2*).

Some in the Putin-era cohort expressed the view that morality in politics boils down to not telling lies (*E1, E4*). But that proposition need not be interpreted as simply telling the whole truth. One put it this way:

[Unlike other professions] politics is a public thing. Its public nature presupposes that you are always expressing your point of view publicly. And if in real life you, being an honorable person, do not lie ... Well, a lie is an obscene, unattractive thing, but you can, we'll say, keep silent about something, understanding that if you were to speak about it, this would not be to the benefit of yourself or your position. Therefore, I, as a politician, always say when I converse with my voters, with people [in general], that I will never lie to you. (*E5*).

In a similar vein, one of his colleagues contended that:

Decency is one of the pivotal things enabling political success. Your views, your principles may not coincide with the principles and views of other people. Moreover, they could be your enemies. But, all the same, it is desirable to designate for others some pivotal point [*sterzhenovoi moment*] and not to tell it to one person in ways different than those you've used to tell it to another ... This doesn't mean that you can't conceal information or that you can't distort information. You can do all of that. But all the same you must not willingly lead another person into a pit (E2).

Finally, nearing the other end of the continuum, the notion of morality as loyalty – referenced by one respondent cited, above, as "clan morality" – was voiced by two members in the sample. In one instance, dishonesty in service to the group was combined with the idea of devotion to a higher good.

> When El'tsin said, "If the cost is increased, I will lie on the railroad tracks," he was sacrificing his own reputation in order to provide protection [kryshu] for the unpopular reforms. Having begun with huge popular approval, he left office with an approval rating of almost zero ... He shielded them [his government] with his own enormous authority, often simply indulging in direct lies. He was required to do this because in politics, more often than in other spheres, a situation arises when you must tell untruths for the benefit of a great cause. Even if his objective was strategic – to go down in Russian history – he understood that he was being evaluated then, and not later. If you're concerned with your reputation today, then you won't earn a reputation in history (C5).

The other respondent referring to morality as loyalty spoke more candidly and directly to the issue. After remarking at some length about the necessary relationship between morality and politics – and then qualifying it in a number of ways by giving examples from his own political experience which required him to forgo the demands of conscience – he seemed to salvage the morality/politics nexus by transforming moral concerns into concrete, *personal* relations. Thus, this respondent, whose entire career has been in law and who expressed great regard for legal principles and practices, illustrated the role of morals in politics by referencing Vladimir Putin's assist-ance to his former superior, the ex-mayor of St. Petersburg, Anatolii

Sobchak, when Sobchak was under indictment for extortion and theft.

> The problem is actually this: if you are to prove your worth, you won't have time to talk about morals in detail. Therefore, in a whole series of actions, it is forgotten, taken for granted, let slip. There are politicians who yield to their friends' requests and those who refuse them. But there is a different example about those who don't refuse their friends about which I will speak openly for the first time to you. Very often when politicians experience difficulties, all the more when these difficulties are of a legal-criminal nature, that's when personal relations in politics appear most clearly. Very often these people's friends disappear.
>
> I had to undertake a legal case connected with the name of the now deceased mayor of St. Petersburg, Anatolii Sobchak. And, certainly, Vladimir Putin, who at that moment had begun to occupy various governmental posts, could have refused him his support. But he didn't do that: he supported Sobchak. I don't know the concrete facts, but in conversation with me Anatolii Sobchak more than once referred to this moral support. And it was very important, although from the point of view of career advancement, it would have been better [for Putin] to refrain from such things ... In just the same way an exceptionally touchy [*ostraya*] situation arose for me, when it would have been more advantageous to terminate his acquaintance with me, but he [Putin] didn't do that and in about two months the situation was straightened out (*E2*).

CONCLUSION

This chapter has explored the relation between politics and morality as voiced by a sample of Russia's political class. It has illustrated the fact that while neither morality nor politics is conceptualized by interview subjects in a uniform way, all subjects express the idea that politics – to one degree or another – should represent a moral undertaking. For the majority of them, including those still active in government and politics, this is clearly not the prevailing situation today. Overwhelmingly, past and present political actors regard politics as a very dirty business, indeed. What is the significance of this negative association between politics and morality in Russian political society? I shall attempt to answer this question by, first, saying a word about variations across specific groups in the sample and, then, conclude with a comment on the apparently larger cultural importance of the politics/morality binary.

As the foregoing analysis has demonstrated, that binary takes a variety of forms: politics versus morality, politics as the means for the realization of moral ends, and various permutations of either term in the binary that modify the significance of each. Although the boundaries separating the cohorts in the present sample are not airtight – owing to the fact that certain subjects assigned to groups politically active at a later time had actually begun their political careers at an earlier date or, conversely, that some included in earlier periods when they held more important posts have continued in politics thereafter – the interview results reported here would none-theless indicate an inverse relationship between proximity to polit-ical power and a full-throated conception of morality. This finding would reinforce the one reported in Chapter 2 in which respondents used the invidious term "clans" for power networks of which they themselves were not members, reserving the more approbatory "teams" for those to which they did belong. Here, the inverse rela-tionship between morality and proximity to power is particularly evident among members of the democratic opposition for whom morality is framed as an absolute value. Although any imputation of causality in this regard would be purely speculative – we cannot know whether moral concerns hindered their political advance or whether their limited success in the sphere of power politics led to reliance on a self-justifying, moral discourse – it seems clear that their narratives feature a politics consumed by morality. They not only reference with pride the principled positions that they have taken on political issues, despite the practical costs, but they cite political defeats and refusals of important positions in the executive, or resignations from them, as examples of commendable behavior. They thereby occupy a specific space on the political spectrum, closest to what one respondent has described as "extreme idealism."

On the other hand, respondents from the Putin-era cohort – those closest to power when these interviews were recorded – rely upon a political discourse approximating "extreme cynicism," at least in the eyes of others. They do not dismiss moral concerns, but they phrase them in the language of flexibility, opportunity and necessity. For them, politics seems to swallow morality. Because their narratives do tend to reflect a sustained engagement with moral issues in the extant political context, their notion of morality is continually up for negotiation and redefinition. They associate morality with telling the truth, then reduce truth-telling to not lying, then to the permissibility of limited deception and, finally, to rendering aid to associates despite legal considerations. These reductions point up the fact that these subjects simultaneously function within a cultural context in which the display of ethical qualities is of paramount importance – along with the opportunity to affirm one's stature by finding moral fault with others (Ries, 1997; Pesmen, 2000) – and within a political context in which formal rules are no substitute for the assistance available through personalized social relations. It is the insolubility of this contradiction that accounts ultimately for the reduction of morality – but not its outright dismissal – to personal or group loyalty.

This contradiction also sheds light on the narratives employed by those comprising the remaining three groups in the sample, which reflect an effort to harmonize moral concerns with political necessities. Like those in the Putin-era group, these respondents stress the import of achieving concrete results through politics, results that admit to some allegedly worthy social purpose. But with a lone exception, and unlike their Putin-era counterparts, the process by which these results are obtained also matters to them. The extreme case, involving the economic reform of the early 1990s, might illustrate this point most effectively. In the absence of any morally defensible procedures for enacting market reforms, privatization and the violent termination of the first post-communist republic, respondents reached beyond the horizons of both morality and politics to summon the spectre of nuclear war, thereby justifying their actions by means of a hyper-semiotic construct casting them in the role of saviors of all humanity.

These narratives on (allegedly) rescuing the world from nuclear annihilation reference more than the justification of particular actions. They also underscore the importance of moral discourse in Russian society and politics. This importance would not seem to lie much in practical action aimed at bringing moral concerns into the political world. As has been shown, most respondents claim that morality plays no role in politics today. Rather, the utility of the discourse of morality consists in the fact that it offers a defense of the self within a noxious environment that seems impervious to the subject's efforts to improve it. Consequently, it might be appropriate to refer to an "absent cause" that sets the discourse of morality in motion, an extra-textual condition "which cannot be unknotted by the operation of pure thought and which must therefore generate a whole more properly narrative apparatus – the text itself – to square its circle and to dispel . . .its intolerable closure" (Jameson, 1981). The absent cause in this case appears to be the extant patterns of social relations bearing on political organization and action, as outlined in Chapter 2, patterns that occlude a public and confine politics to the arena of power networks. Moreover, these patterns are reflected in the ontology of the political class discussed in Chapter 3, especially in narratives of "the people," who are portrayed as inert and subject to manipulation. These images require altruistic champions to accomplish that which "the people" cannot themselves do and to protect them from the manipulation of unscrupulous others. Traces of these social relations and of the ontology accompanying and supporting them appear in some of the respondents' narratives:

• I think that Russia needs European-style social democracy . . . [But] our society has a big percentage of poor people. And what kind of democracy can there be among the indigent? For an indigent, there is no democracy whatsoever. He is only given to drink, to munch on a cucumber and to sleep somewhere under a fence. He spits on everything else (A4).

- There is nothing better than democracy for individuals inclined toward self-government. But democracy for a herd of sheep is unthinkable. Democracy in a narcotics, alcohol or gambling den is unthinkable ... Society itself has changed, and not for the better. From the point of view of representing their demands to the authorities, even the ability to make demands, society has degraded (D2).

- What has hindered me from achieving my objectives in politics? The thousand-year history of Russia, that's what (D6).

In the face of these perceptions of the social context, morality in politics as a categorical imperative, as an embrace of impersonal norms, seems doomed from the outset. In its place stands another variety of morality, congruent with actual social relations: morality as loyalty to one's confederates – "clan morality." However, this particular moral practice does not expunge the principled or impersonal form of morality from political consciousness. That version of morality remains for many as an element central to their professed identity, one articulated through a discourse invidiously distinguishing the self from the shameful other.

5 Competence

In any activity it is necessary to be a professional (*B9*).

The words "professional" and "professionalism" enjoy an almost magical ring in Russian political parlance. They are often intoned as a panacea setting right any number of enumerated ills. They connote a mastery of affairs and thus are sought-for things commonly regarded to be woefully absent in the world of practical endeavors. "Professional" thus contributes to political discourse the quality of competence. However, it also admits to quite different definitions in the Russian context, sometimes opposing the idea of politics, sometimes coinciding with it. This polysemic quality of "professional" appears to be of critical import for drawing divisions and constructing group identities in the world of politics. This chapter seeks to determine how the word "professional" has been used by past and present members of Russia's political class and outlines two opposing narrative programs that constitute its meanings. It also has a secondary objective: *viz.*, to frame the results reported, here, within the scope of a dynamic model of change in Soviet, and now Russian, political communication. Because these objectives are analytically distinct, I return to the second one only in conclusion.

DISCOURSES OF PROFESSIONALISM AND POLITICS

In all, some twenty-one of the thirty-four members of the sample used "professional(ism)" during interviews. In twelve instances, it was self-referential, connoting their membership in some profession outside of politics. Accordingly, this group is a subset of what can be called "professionals in politics." In seven other cases, its usage served to include the respondent in a group called "political professionals" or "professional politicians." In the final two instances, the respondent, while not referring to himself either as a professional politician or as someone who entered politics from some outside professional career, denoted a class of professional politicians of which he was not a member.

The focus, here, falls first on those twelve respondents referring to themselves as professionals who had entered politics after establishing careers in other fields. Quite naturally, these individuals emphasized the element of substantive knowledge available to themselves because of their previous endeavors. Particularly among those who entered politics from academic backgrounds, professionalism represented for them a much-needed antidote to a cloistered, bureaucratic culture pervading government, not to mention the reckless ignorance displayed by politicians themselves. Emblematically, one commented on how his professional background had enabled him to view issues more perspicaciously than could others around him (D5). Another went so far as to say that, as an economist, it had been impossible for him to countenance working within the Soviet system – in his professional eyes, "it was simply absurd." He later resigned from El'tsin's government for the same expressed reason (D6). Important from this general perspective was the sort of disorder and incompetence that those from professional backgrounds claimed to have noticed when they assumed governmental responsibilities. Along these lines, a third respondent remarked that on joining the Administration of the President, he became "very despondent because of the low effectiveness of the political actions of the authorities, [seeing there] a huge number of complete blunders, an enormous number of ill-considered decisions taken by dilettantes" (C6). On becoming a staffer in the national legislature, a fourth found himself doing political work because a great number of the legislators "were not involved in any political activities but were in general occupied with things of which I could make neither head nor tail" (C4). Facing similar circumstances, a fifth prided himself and his colleagues on bringing an anti-bureaucratic cast of mind to the corridors of power. "Although we didn't know any bureaucratic games," he remarked, "decisions were taken quickly, operationally and effectively. Although we had to contend with a bumbling bureaucracy – maybe even one intent on sabotaging our program – we made the bureaucratic wheels spin a thousand times faster than they do today" (B9).

Respondents who had come to government service from non-political backgrounds tended rather uniformly to cast themselves in the Promethean role of bringing knowledge to an otherwise fumbling and/or stolid bureaucracy lacking even a trace of intelligent direction. They regularly employed the term "professional" – and its many surrogates: expert, specialist, brains and so on – to signal their distance from, and their intention to harness, that bureaucracy. For them, "professional" seemed to function in two important respects: first, as an empty signifier enabling group identity and political action; second, as a claim to cultural capital that can exchange for political power. These two functions of "professionalism" underpin a discourse admitting to internal inconsistency and ambiguity, as well as to a semantic flexibility that enables the term to perform a social function of marking its bearers in two important ways.

The first marking tends toward associativity. That is, "professional" functions as an "empty signifier" – a term coined (to my knowledge) by Roland Barthes (1972) that has been further developed by Ernesto Laclau in his theory of politics. In a playfully serious vein, Barthes describes a process by which ordinary signifiers can be impressed into the service of creating everyday myths by hollowing out their signifieds and filling them with new ones. For instance, the signifier "sexuality" might be emptied of its semantic content and then supplied with "aftershave lotion" as is done in commercial advertising. As such, the first signifier, "sexuality," becomes then a signifier of the second one, "aftershave lotion," the mythic message now reading: "this aftershave lotion is a guarantee of sexual success." Naturally, the very fact that it is possible to talk about this process illustrates that the terms "sexuality" and "aftershave lotion" have not somehow lost their meanings or have become identical. Rather, signifiers get emptied because of their relations to other terms in a given discourse in which those signifiers appear, in this case in the discourse of commercial advertising.

Laclau has taken this insight further, into the arena of politics, noting how an empty signifier can establish a discursive horizon, a semantic space shared by a community of speakers. It thus creates an inclusive "we." This usage – "professional" indexing a (potentially) universal class – is evident among the respondents, one of whom put it very directly by saying that "in any activity it is necessary to be a professional" (B9). An empty signifier is able to create this inclusive "we" precisely because it is a word voided of significance, emptied of any particular meaning, detached from any signifieds, and therefore ready to be appropriated by subjects who would use it as a pivot around which their narrative program can be organized. Laclau emphasizes the fact that the process of emptying the term of its normal significance is critical to this operation, inasmuch as such a signifier is then able to express meanings beyond those transmissible by its ("unemptied") counterpart in ordinary language. It thus represents a form of catachresis, a figurative term that cannot be substituted for by a literal one. In the quotidian world of politics, such terms as "the people," "freedom" and "justice" would exemplify empty signifiers. Each can function to evoke a political community representing a totality constructed on the basis of equivalence and difference. Within the discourse of "the people," for instance, each act of signification includes both equivalencies, connoting membership in this construct, and differences between it and anti-popular or opposing forces providing the distinction or boundary necessary to constitute "the people." As such, an empty signifier indexes something that is both impossible and necessary: impossible, because it cannot reference a fully inclusive "we" – in our instance, because it distinguishes a group and its activities from others betraying an "absence of professionalism" or those described as "unprofessional" – yet necessary, because the term performs as a predicate for ordering the world, that totality enacted by and through the discourse (Laclau, 2005,

Laclau and Mouffe, 2001; Torfing, 1999; Howarth *et al.*, 2000). The characteristics associated with emptiness – breadth, ambiguity, opacity and contradiction – are amply present in the discourse of professionals in politics. Their import, again, does not consist in logical coherence but in the nebulous associations that their purveyors want their audiences to think about (Barthes, 1972). In this way, syntagmatic associations encoded in the word "professional" can displace its semantic content in actual communicative practice (Lotman, 1990).

The second marking tends toward distinction. It creates an exclusive "we," professionals, who have a special claim to knowledge and ethics. It thereby represents a form of cultural capital in possession of some group who can exchange it for other forms of capital – in our instance, for political capital. Because cultural capital is embodied – it cannot be disassociated from its bearer as could, say, economic capital – professionals in politics claim the right to power and influence not because of popular endorsement but simply because of who they are (Bourdieu, 1986). This claim is advanced in two ways. First, its usage constitutes an imagined beacon in the foggy seas of Russian politics, lighting some visage of direction and destination for the ship of state. It implies that the prevailing situation can be regarded as a set of problems to be solved, and that professionals are required to solve them. Second, this claim to a special knowledge needed to resolve common problems already carries a trace of the term's other dimension: disinterestedness. Here, the professional symbolically stands aside from the flesh-and-blood struggles of the political world and assumes a purely benevolent posture toward that world. Just as, say, a dentist is not interested *qua* dentist whether he or she is applying her skills in the mouths of relatives, friends, strangers or enemies, so the professional in the world of politics can be relied upon to lend his/her expertise where it is needed, owing to no other motivation than a strictly "professional" one (Bourdieu, 1984). The Russian political world portrayed by many of the respondents – one filled with ruthlessness, duplicity and intrigues – would seem to place a premium on this aspect of the term. Whereas most others potentially mean harm to oneself and associates, professionals imply help. Whereas most others cannot be trusted, professionals can. Thus, a discourse of morality is grafted onto that of expertise, inviting the addressee to associate "the professional" with "the good" (Edelman, 1988; Lazar and Lazar, 2004), thus forming a nodal point where the discourses of competence and morality intertwine (Laclau, 2005). Taken together, these dimensions of "professional" as discussed in the present context – that is, expert knowledge plus ethics – constitute the cultural capital of outsiders entering the field of politics. In order to bolster their stocks of this capital, they are given either to denying the term "professional" to others on that field or to denigrating the forms of capital – economic, social and political – that they possess.

THE DISCOURSE OF PROFESSIONALS IN POLITICS

Although discursive strategies built around "professional(ism)" are apparent for that group of respondents entering government from non-political backgrounds, it is particularly pronounced for four members of the sample who worked as an identifiable team in the Administration of the President in the mid-1990s under Boris El'tsin. I therefore rely, here, primarily on their responses in order to present a concentrated expression of this discourse, showing how it both provides a claim to cultural capital and, thus, access to the political field, and functions as an empty signifier enabling group identity, purpose and action. Although respondents shifted from one office to another within its various – often reorganized – divisions, I shall treat them all simply as a team of individuals working in the Administration of the President who prepared policy proposals for El'tsin, who were in direct and often daily contact with him, who acted in some matters in his stead while he was ill or otherwise incapacitated (Baturin et al., 2001), and who involved themselves directly in the partisan politics of the electoral process.

As described in interviews, their paths to high office were exceptional inasmuch as personal ties were only of secondary importance in their recruitment. One, a political scientist turned presidential speechwriter, joined El'tsin's circle during the 1990 election campaign for the Russian Congress of People's Deputies. As described by a member of this group, the others were recruited by presidential aides who

> by the end of 1992 had realized that the situation had spun out of control and that they needed help. From the point of view of career politicians, career *chinovniki*, this unstable, unpredictable period required people of another type, intellectuals, to use the Western word, who were able to help reorient [the presidency] in this unstable, unpredictable situation.
>
> In those days there were a lot of public affairs shows on television and I happened to appear quite often on them. El'tsin's people saw me and asked me to join the administration. You see, El'tsin regarded the Seventh Congress of People's Deputies of the Russian Federation [December 1992 – M. U.] as a big defeat for himself and he was unsatisfied with the shape of his team and with the way that they had prepared their moves for this Congress. Hence, the idea arose to form a team of advisors ... to put in professionals. So, El'tsin's people began to gather such a team according to the following algorithm: those who appear on public affairs shows on television, those who appear in the press, are publicly acknowledged to be outstanding professionals ... They invited such people to the Kremlin for conversations. If the results were positive, they would tell the candidate that they were forming a new presidential team and invite him to join ... And they asked these experts if they had someone whom they could recommend, some of whom were subsequently recruited ... At first, we were simply a council of experts giving advice to the president. But after a while, a number of us took full-time jobs in the Administration of the President ... To meet the extraordinary situation, we simply had to gather professionals because of the crisis (C3).

Of particular note in these remarks would be the discourse of disinterested expertise underlying the entire recruitment process: the selection of those "publicly regarded to be outstanding professionals." Placing a premium on such public intellectuals seems to be incongruent with the narrowly political crisis – a legislative backlash, poorly handled, against the government of Egor Gaidar and its policy of "shock therapy" – said to have required the summoning of professional help. Why would this trigger a need to call in outside professionals? What do historians, geographers, economists, ethnicity specialists and so forth know about managing votes in the national legislature? A second incongruity involves the shifting of positions from experts to de facto policymakers in which some in this group reported to be involved. In both instances, "professionalism" would refer neither to expert knowledge bearing on matters at hand, nor back to itself as a knowledge proper to its own object, because in context such would be irrelevant. Having thus been emptied of content, "professionalism" in this instance has become an empty signifier affirming group identity and purpose.

In consonance with the respondents' emphasis on professionalism, these interviews were peppered with metaphors for the group such as "new brains with new ideas" (C6), a "brain center" and an "intellectual machine" (C5), and a "smart Jew next to the ruler" (C3). They reported being well received by career officials in the government who good-naturedly referred to them as "egg-heads" (C3). One remarked on this by noting that El'tsin would often say to others:

> "Here are my brains." And when he would refer to us as his brains, I could feel this myself. For instance, on one occasion there was a visit by representatives from another state and we were in the receiving line outdoors and it began to rain. Pavel Grachev [Minister of Defense – M. U.] was standing not far from me and came over immediately when the rain started, opening his umbrella. And he said, "Please, let me cover you up. We can't afford to let the brains get wet" (C1).

Counterposed to these comments on the import of professional knowledge for improving government, a counter-narrative appears in the responses of this group concerning the actual, and problematic, application of that knowledge itself. Although some claimed specific successes, especially on certain matters for which the help of outside experts could also be enlisted to overcome the torpid performances of career officials (C3), a more frequent response suggested a more-or-less constant scramble to try to stay abreast of pressing issues. Rather than working out rational policies for the government to pursue, one member of the group likened himself to a "shoemaker with a lot of clients." Although he was already overburdened with their orders, he felt unable to refuse to take on new customers. Thus, he was forced to neglect policy matters and additionally found his efforts hampered by "a deficit of technology in the face of a fantastic number of ongoing problems [that he was required to address. He complained that he] did not have the technology to anticipate them and thus begin to solve these problems before they had created a storm around us" (C3).

One of his colleagues lamented generally the conditions prevailing in the Administration of the President, noting that:

> On one hand, the presence of new brains, unburdened by any kind of Communist notions, was a good thing. But on the other hand, it was very bad because these people were completely not organizationally oriented [ne apparatnye] and they didn't know how to write proper documents [kachestvennye apparatnye bumagi]. And they were unable to write documents on time. So this machine, composed of new people – at any rate, at the top – who were not professional chinovniki, was unable to work effectively. At lower levels there were some representatives of the old apparatus. They grumbled, and they would do some things which were organizationally competent. But by their nature they simply didn't understand what was expected of them (C6).

This predicament – professionals in charge who lacked the skills to manage their respective situations – was also iterated obliquely by professional economists who had served in the reform government of the early 1990s:

- You can't study how the political process is constructed under the conditions of the collapse of one regime and the absence of institutions in another. You won't read about this in books. My experience shows that books don't teach everything (*B8*).

• Many things were dictated not by some abstract economic theory or by the Chicago School of [Milton] Friedman – although they had christened us the " Chicago boys" – but simply by concrete situations (*B9*).

Despite the fact that three of the four respondents who had worked in the Administration of the President explicitly opposed professionalism to politics, their comments nonetheless gestured toward the necessity of having a "feel for the game" of politics (Bourdieu, 1977, 1984) that they had not appreciated earlier. One put it this way:

> The work is hard. Very hard. Because every day you must somehow give recommendations on a very big number of questions that you haven't always sorted out by a long shot. This is inescapable.
> If these are your duties, you must be not so much an expert in a certain field, but more of a systems expert, *being able to feel intuitively what's important, what's not, or to what to direct your attention and what not to.* This is fatiguing. It's hard particularly when you're not accustomed to it. Overall, there is this intellectual assembly line [*konveier*] that doesn't stop for a minute and is impossible to escape (*C6*).

The lacuna for the professional in government can be filled, these remarks indicate, by acquiring the same political capacities that the discourse of professionalism itself constructs *in opposition to* the professional's identity. Two other members of this group reported having comparable experiences.

> After [leaving government service], and filling the gaps in my education, I now understand things that could have helped me then. I'll give you a concrete example. One of my jobs concerned the problem of corruption in Russia. And when I joined El'tsin's administration, mine was an absolutely common-sense, everyday concept of corruption ... So I invited to my office the first deputy

heads of all the force-wielding agencies: the Procuracy, the MVD, the FSK (now it's called the FSB). And I asked them whether they knew about that operation in the USA at the end of the seventies when FBI agents, posing as Arab sheiks, caught out a number of senators. A scandal ensued, and a day of reckoning, after which a more-or-less serious anti-corruption policy was begun in the USA. "What do you think?" I asked, "Could we conduct a similar operation in Russia?" They began to huddle together, exchanging glances. Then they began to say that, of course, this would be good, but it would contravene [existing] legislation. And they all looked so dejected that I quickly began to understand: they are not so much looking for the means to solve a problem as they are arguments not to solve it (C3).

Similarly, one of his colleagues lamented that:

We were all creative people but we were completely unable to do the organizational work that would put our projects into some kind of concrete practice ... Now I know how I should have conducted myself. I had enormous opportunities. I had a huge, four-window office with a view of the Kremlin. And all the *chinovniki* were very afraid of the Presidential Council, because the president was very closed off, and we often met with him one-to-one. And they all thought we could request apartments from him, pay raises and, the main thing, we could get him to sign a complaint against the Rector of Moscow University or any other big official like that which would remove him from office straightaway ... The *chinovniki* thought that we could do this quite easily and so our abilities to influence them were enormous. But I didn't use them ... When you go up to a *chinovnik* and say that something is important for the country ... well. No, you tell him about his personal place in the project that you're proposing. If you are thinking about the interests of the country, then be so good as to convince the *chinovnik*. That is the direct path to success. And this isn't cynicism, it's right (C5).

These remarks suggest another notion of professionalism present in the narratives of many respondents: professional politics as know-how, a capacity for political-administrative management and direction. Some, such as *B9*, in remarks quoted above, seemed to fuse it with a concomitant emphasis on substantive expertise, but *B9* admitted that he and his associates "never understood the rules of bureaucratic play." Nor do they seem to have been much disposed to do so because entering that world would constitute a direct threat to the professional identities constituted by their discourse and the influence – based on knowledge and disinterestedness – provided them in the political world by maintaining that posture. Thus, these political outsiders continued to distance themselves from politics. Adopting a relatively mild version of this discourse, one respondent remarked that:

> Politics is a rather boring profession in normal times. There's nothing interesting about sitting in the Duma from day to day with nothing going on. Or sitting in the government. It's all humdrum. And that's politics in any country – Denmark, Sweden or contemporary Russia ... Politics [means] in general from whom to take money and with whom to share it out. Of course, there are people who like to do this, but I myself don't relate to such things (*B5*).

Adding a somewhat sharper edge, another disclaimed an interest in present-day politics owing to its bureaucratization.

> Today, the political and the bureaucratic-administrative are indivisible. If two ministers are quarrelling about their spheres of competence – a purely bureaucratic flap – then all the newspapers will be writing about political contradictions. That is, they'll call that political. And against that backdrop real politics has simply gone. It doesn't exist because the institutions are not arguing with one another. [Political] parties more contend over bureaucratic things – who gets what post? Who pushes himself forward? – and not about the actuality of their activities (*C4*).

With yet a sharper edge to his comments, a third respondent regarded professional politics in Russia generally as some self-satisfying cynicism indifferent to any moral limits. Some of his remarks in this vein – concerning "clan morality," theft as loyalty, and the pride taken by today's "professional" politicians in their cynicism – have already been quoted in the preceding chapter. In words recalling the notion of "know-how" as knowledge of how to break the rules (Ledeneva, 2006), he went on to say that these professional politicians display:

> absolutely technological thinking. I see the goal and I don't see impediments . . . We have a job to do. I have resources. I effectively deploy them to achieve the goal. And to do that, we'll say, I lie. But that's the technology! Today I was saying one thing, tomorrow [it will be] another. The ensemble of these "professional" activities is politics. It means that politics is a dirty thing . . . And the end results are all dirt (C6).

These remarks reference a graft of moral discourse onto that of professionalism, resulting in a sharp distinction between "real" professionals and "political" professionals for whom *lying* is a part of their technology. However, those relying on this discourse of professionalism sometimes would abandon moral concerns when speaking of actual political events in which they were involved. For example, two respondents who had served in the Administration of the President called particular attention to the political burdens shouldered by Boris El'tsin in protecting them and others from public criticism (C1; C5). The remarks of one on this score have already been quoted in the preceding chapter, but they bear repeating in the present context.

> When El'tsin said, "If the cost is increased, I will lie on the railroad tracks," he was sacrificing his own reputation in order to provide protection [*kryshu*] to the unpopular reforms. Having begun with huge popular approval, he left office with an approval rating of almost zero . . . He shielded them [his government] with his own

enormous authority, often simply indulging in direct lies. He was required to do so because in politics, more often than in other spheres, a situation arises in which you must tell untruths for the benefit of a great cause (C5).

These comments are an instance of code switching. They illustrate how actors sometimes draw on an opposing discourse in order to make sense of things around them. Importantly, here they are directed toward another actor, El'tsin, and consequently do not impugn the identity of the professional in politics for whom the discourse of professionalism remains central. As one member of the Administration of the President put it:

> We spoke with the president without a hidden agenda for our own careers but said what we thought, based on our knowledge and experience. In this respect there is a peculiar effect: there are, for instance, scholarly ethics, and a scholar in his own sphere cannot transgress against the principles of scholarly ethics. As a professional, I cannot lie. As a matter of fact, this translates into politics. I am unable to be cunning. I thought that sending the army to Chechnya would be harmful, and I said so. [Respondent then named three colleagues in the Administration of the President who did likewise and referred to "others" there who also did so – M. U.]. And this is not so much [a matter of] political ethics but a continuation of scholarly ethics and their moral principles (C3).

Remarks such as these might be interpreted as discursive strategies aimed to husband the cultural capital of professionals in politics by valorizing truth-telling, a form of that disinterestedness from which their cultural capital in part derives. They seem to be saying that they care not to advance their fortunes by telling others – especially power – what they might want to hear. They do not disguise the truth because of some interest; they tell the truth precisely because they are disinterested.

THE DISCOURSE OF PROFESSIONAL POLITICIANS

The obverse side of self-described disinterestedness among professionals in politics would be represented, of course, by the imputation of base motives and/or nefarious acts to others, especially to professional politicians. In the sample, such disparaging comments on the profession of politics were – with two exceptions – confined to those in the El'tsin administrations and to the oppositional democrats. One of these exceptions executed a conceptual reversal of the negative stereotype of the political professional, waxing abstractly but rhapsodically about such an individual's distinctive skills and qualities and thus fashioning him as an imagined replacement for the flesh-and-blood professional politicians of today.[1] The other, who served in the first El'tsin government, had been active in the dissident movement during Soviet times, an experience that had impressed on him the fecklessness of moral rigidity in conducting practical political affairs once he had become a state official. He noted that:

> a politician bears a responsibility other than morality, and people who enter politics need rather different qualities. All the time they are required to take decisions that have no basis in morality, enabling them to evaluate and choose. All the time they have to weigh things. And it is senseless to evaluate the conduct simply on moral grounds. That's the conclusion that I reached . . . But there is a threshold that one mustn't cross. In particular, one mustn't apply torture and so on. But what can you do with that theory? Who will listen to you? If a terrorist falls into the hands of the Federal Security Services, and they know that this person has knowledge

---

[1] The exception is B4 who himself had entered politics from an academic background. His construction of the "professional politician," however, seems to betray that background itself inasmuch as it concerns not the present political class but a new species of political actor required by the conditions of the twenty-first century. For B4, then, the professional politician must display "developed, cultured thinking" and have a developed feeling for "artistic imagination." Furthermore he or she must have "the talent to be liked, to attract attention and sympathy [plus] the ability to take responsibility under conditions in which others would not . [He or she] must be a political sage, a *politosoph.*"

about a bomb set to explode in two hours, will they torture him? They will. If they didn't, they would be sacked for being unprofessional and guilty for those who perished (*B*2).

Those from the Gorbachev and Putin cohorts tended to see things comparably, searching for some way to harmonize the demands of conscience and the exigencies of politics. For example, one from the Gorbachev group configured professionalism and morality around goals, "not according to the process of decision making [wherein lies are told or personal agendas pursued] but according to the actual results and effects of decisions on the polity." Drawing on the example of the First Chechen War, he argued that:

> Any war in Chechnya is disgraceful and dishonorable ... El'tsin unleashed this war in Chechnya when he could have just tried to understand Dudaev [his opponent, then president of Chechnya – M. U.]. He could have called Dudaev and said, "Listen, you're a mountaineer! You're an honorable man. Well, let's get together and think a bit about why you have to leave [the Russian Federation]. What do you think, for what? This isn't necessary. Let's put our heads together." He could have solved it all. But instead of healing his nose, he cut it off. And his people said, "In two days we'll solve the whole problem with one regiment." That's what they did upstairs – well, how to say it? – they took an unprofessional, immoral decision so casually (*A*4).

Another member of that cohort, describing his past self as a professional politician, recounted the Gorbachev team's efforts to undo the "totalitarianism and dogmatism" that had dogged the Soviet Union, only to be pushed aside by El'tsin's reformers dogmatically insisting on their total plan for an immediate rush into a market economy. He then likened the Putin regime to Russia's last tsar who wrote in his diary on the day of the Revolution that swept him from power that

> "the sky is blue, the birds are singing and things are fine all around. And at the front, things are likewise more or less okay" ... Although

I am an opponent of the authorities, I would very much hope that they can pass through the terrible ordeal brought about by prosperous times, when the feeling begins to take shape that all is going well. This is particularly [problematic] when all of the mass media – which they've taken into their own hands – are saying the same thing, and with the agreement with the entire parliament and Council of the Federation, with the agreement of all the governors – this is a huge, colossal danger ... Who was it who said, "If it seems to you that all goes well, then there's something that you haven't noticed"? I have just that sense, that the Russian leadership has convinced itself that everything's fine and has created just this situation of complacency, this rot in every crevice ... They criticize [the authorities] for not permitting freedom of speech, which is bad for people because they then can't express themselves. And that's all true. But that's not the most terrible danger. The most terrible one lies in the fact that they have deprived themselves of an objective perception of the situation, the one that they're actually in (A2).

This suspension of the play of politics was emphasized by a third member of this group as necessarily resulting in "stupidity ... For a politician must have a strong character and intellectual flexibility." He went on to say that a politician has:

the ability to calculate his moves, like a chess player, and to find non-standard solutions, like a poet who is having trouble finding the right rhyme ... The most paradoxical thing is that diplomacy [the field in which the respondent had worked – M. U.] must be honest, but that doesn't mean that everything gets said or said just so. It doesn't mean to lie, but more like holding back [certain things]. The parties to negotiations must understand one another and one another's goals and interests, otherwise progress is impossible (A1).

Noteworthy, here, would be the metaphorical construction of politics distinguishing these respondents' concept of the political from those of the professionals in politics. If the latter's understanding takes its cues from their backgrounds in the academic world whose discourse emphasizes knowledge and truth, those from the Gorbachev cohort draw on the metaphors of play. This is particularly evident in the remarks of $A1$, likening a politician to a chess player, or to a poet looking for unusual solutions in his prosody. But it is likewise apparent in $A4$'s remarks about the politician's duty to understand his opponent and to approach him in the most advantageous way, suggesting the critical importance of a "feel for the game." Moreover, $A2$'s emphasis on competition in the political arena as something necessary to avoid blindness and blunders leading to great tragedy also reflects this "feel for the game" characteristic of the discourse of this group.

The comments from the Putin cohort generally tended to dovetail with those in the Gorbachev group with respect to politics as a profession unto itself. But they also had something of a keener edge to them, perhaps reflecting more the rough-and-tumble world of the contemporary Russian milieu rather than the relative refinement of the *perestroika* era. Echoing the abstract remarks of one in the Gorbachev group that politics is principally a struggle for power ($A4$), one member of the Putin cohort concretized the "facts of political life" in some detail, mentioning horse-trading, intimidation and the use of raw power, itself. He displayed no apprehension in so doing, regarding these *political* phenomena as "normal" ($E4$). Another described politics as "a profession, like a taxi-driver or a journalist" and in vivid contrast to those from the El'tsin sample uncoupled moral principles from professional ones, arguing that it is individuals rather than professions that are moral or immoral. Thus, for a professional politician, he allowed that morals may have to be sacrificed in order to accomplish the basic purpose of the profession itself: namely, to get "results" ($E5$). Results, in turn, are governed by criteria specific to the profession of politics. As if echoing Weber's concept, cited above, of politics implying "distance to things and men," he noted that:

> the main thing in politics is the ability to find agreement [with others]. I am two different persons in politics and in [everyday] life.

That is, in life I am impulsive, sometimes uncompromising, and often emotions get the upper hand over reason. But all the same in politics for me it's just the reverse. I know very well that you can't give in to emotions, you can't let emotions govern your head ... Politics, then, is the ability to walk between the raindrops, to walk through the raindrops and stay dry (E5).

A third member of this cohort called attention to the importance of abstracting oneself from immediate conditions in order to achieve success in politics.

It has been my job to advance the causes of very different people: democrats and non-democrats ... practically the entire spectrum of actors who names have been on the first pages of the press. But when representing their interests, I have tried never to profit from acquaintance with them nor from the fact that I'm working for their cause ... But you can't explain this as altruism; it's just a condition of successful work. And nothing more (E2).

He went on to point out that politics is a process "entirely transpiring through groups of people, groups of interests." Unlike stable societies where these groups are known to others, in Russia they all function "within closed regimes, and this is well known ... Unanticipated groups, unexpected teams or sub-teams might arise [at any time] pursuing their own interests [and thus making] the course of political life unknown and unpredictable" (E2). He noted that this confusion is characteristic of the legislative process with which he is involved.

My work involves concrete texts, bringing them to life in society, building the Russian state. There is, you see, a closed process of evaluation that goes on, in particular, in this office. While the words only lie on paper, there is a process by which they are interpreted ... what, for instance, goes out in the press or what political commentators have to say. Sometimes the thought that you have inserted comes out completely otherwise in public [discussions] of politics ... And it is an absolute lie [to assert] that the activity of the Duma is predetermined [by the Kremlin]. I know the activities of the Duma from the inside ... Legal drafts are birthed in the Duma, and by 723 other people with the right of legislative initiative who introduce them and battle for their drafts. There are a lot of contradictions in these texts and they have to be resolved. The process is interesting ... Of course there is an absence of time [for all of this]. Things, people move very fast with no time simply to sit awhile and think. [Consequently] this very often leads to a superficial solution to problems and therefore to so many harsh policy decisions that have a negative influence on the fate of many people. And simply legislators have not had the opportunity to speak with others and understand the opposing point of view ... So I think that for whatever reason in a given situation [there may be] an absence of flexibility, and you have to search for the reason in yourself ... There is an element of self-love that exists in every person: the main thing is how to control it and not to make yourself out to be something great (E2).

The construction of a profession of politics by those in the Putin cohort much resembles the discourse of those in the Gorbachev group, just as it sets them apart from the orientation of El'tsin's disinterested experts. On one hand, they portray politics as a tricky process ("to walk between the raindrops") surrounded by uncertainty and unpredictability, not unlike the "feel-for-the-game" orientation of the perestroika-era respondents. This seems a far cry, indeed, from those coming to politics from academic backgrounds who confess a lack of understanding of these matters and who perceived things through the prism of their own professional life such that the quest for certainty – both factual and moral – structures their narratives.

On the other hand, members of the Putin group, again like those from Gorbachev's time, seem relatively reconciled to the imperfections in the process itself. In contrast both to the opposition democrats and to those from academic backgrounds who had joined El'tsin's government, they do not valorize truth and morality as consummate standards for assessing political action, suggesting their reliance on social and political, rather than on cultural, capital. They call attention to negative features of the political process and express concern for making improvements in it, but what seems to distinguish them from all others in the sample is that, with a single exception,[2] one finds no trace in their narratives of the notion that the state is required to achieve some larger social purpose. Unlike seventeen of their Gorbachev and El'tsin-era counterparts who did so explicitly, they tend not to organize their narratives around the idea of a state-directed project – *perestroika* or reform – whose success can be measured in social improvements. Rather, Putin-era respondents would concur only in part with a definition of political action put forth by one member of the Gorbachev team who referred to it as a combination of "know-how," "cynicism" and a conscience guided by "the goal attainment of moral ends" (*A1*). But political identities of the Putin-era group seem not to hinge on social projects. Commenting on this matter, one respondent argued that currently "we have no image of the future. No one is even thinking about it. Now, more often, we just have images of the past" (*C4*). Along those lines, the remarks of one of the respondents from the Putin-era cohort are instructive:

> a market economy is a necessity [for Russia]. To make this
> practical means to adapt it to Russian circumstances which,
> above all, means to study the experience of our own people – an
> experience which is certainly filled with prejudices and shortcomings.
> But we must study that history, not ignore it. The main thing is
> to understand that we are doing this not for the sake of the
> West, not for the sake of making America happy, but are following
> in the footsteps of Peter the First and Katherine the Second
> who emulated the West for the sake of Russia ... [So we must]

---

[2] The person in question, *E3*, may be the exception that shows the rule. Both a background as an anarchist activist and, later, as a labor-oriented politician provide him with the credentials that he brings to the governing party, United Russia, as the leader of its left wing.

speak about these things in a way that can form a consensus around Putin's point of view. Consensus is more important than voting, because in Russia you have *sobornost'* [a mystical communion of the population – M. U.] as a form of democracy. Leaders are not really free but exist within the framework of definite representations. To depart from that framework is to destroy the program (*E3*).

As are those from another member of that cohort, quoted in the preceding chapter in another context, which are also relevant to this one:

One must lean on the old. On the experience of the Soviet Union and a thousand years of Russia ... On our traditions such as communalism, mutual aid and collectivism ... Even if one wanted to transplant the Protestant ethic to our soil, it wouldn't work ... Our tradition is that the state is mama and papa. That's good or bad; but it's our tradition! (*E5*).

Thus it seems that, for exponents of this version of political discourse, individuals see themselves as living in the here-and-now, rather than in some imagined future. They are in the game and it is the game that constructs their identities as "professional politicians."

CONCLUSION

This discussion of professionalism and politics leads to two principal conclusions: (1) that the discourse of competence evident in the narratives of Russia's political class appears in two opposing variants; and (2) that over the period from *perestroika* to the present, a revolution – in the original sense of that term (Arendt, [1963] 1982) – has occurred whereby things, having left their earlier state, have after an interlude returned to it. Taking these points in order, it is possible to identify both a discourse employed by professionals in politics and another used by professional politicians. The major terms in each, and their mutual oppositions, are set out in Table 5.1. The columns in the table are constructed as binaries in order to illustrate the pure forms of each discursive structure. However, as this chapter has shown, respondents – although relying

Table 5.1 *Analytic distinctions between the discourse of professionals in politics and the discourse of professional politicians*

Discourse of professionals in politics	Discourse of professional politicians
substantive knowledge	know-how
process-situated ethics	results-oriented ethics
problem solving	problem managing
order bringing	disorder negotiated
social purpose emphasized	social context emphasized
must be oneself	must abstract from oneself

primarily on one of these discourses – tend to shift on occasion to the other one. That result at the narrative level does not cancel discursive differences. It merely records the fact that at least two discourses of professionalism are available to members of the political class and that they sometimes draw from both.

The play of these discourses in Russian politics and their predominance among one or another section of political actors reflects the various capitals deployed on the field of politics: cultural capital based on expert knowledge and ethics among professionals in politics, and that social and political capital pertinent to professional politicians according to whom know-how and results are paramount. Consequently, those whose claim to, or on, power is based on cultural capital emphasize both the social purpose served by their actions (disinterestedness) and the embodied aspect of that capital itself. *They must be themselves*, true to their professional standards and ethics. For professional politicians, however, these same vectors tend to be reversed. Doing politics seems to be uppermost for them, and at critical junctures, this requires that *they not be themselves*. These two forms of capital also appear to account for the differing social ontologies pertinent to these discourses. Whereas for professionals in politics the world is composed of problems that they have been commissioned to solve as well as disorder that they have been summoned to set aright, for professional politicians imperfection attends the world around them. Problems can be contained, minimized, managed, but not eradicated; disorder to one degree or another is a constant with which one must reckon.

The presence of these competing discourses on Russia's political field provides ample room for misunderstanding among political actors and tends to amplify animosities among them. Take for instance the question of social purpose. All those who worked in either the first or second El'tsin administration are identified with its principal domestic program, the introduction of capitalism. This reform was legitimized by the cultural capital of the reformers themselves: "professional economics" (Lvov, 1991; Leont'ev, 1991a, 1991b). But they also appended a paradoxical moral component to it. In the words of an oppositional democrat:

> These people, [Egor] Gaidar and his team, were above all
> anti-communists. They therefore approached their politics in an
> explicitly *amoral* way. Why amoral? Because they regarded all the
> misfortunes and calamities of communism as stemming from its
> attempt to fulfill a moral program with the use of state power.
> They would say: "When the discussion concerns morals in politics,
> it smells of the concentration camp" (*D1*).

From the perspective of professionals in power, there is a certain, albeit paradoxical, logic at work in this injunction: *viz.*, accomplish a social purpose – the creation of capitalism – which must, for morality's sake, be pursued outside of any moral considerations. This logic, however, does not translate into political discourse in which contingency, uncertainty and, in the end, morality all enter. Pursuing such an agenda invites others to take umbrage, as the above-quoted remarks would suggest.

At first blush, then, the debilitating problems of communication evident in post-Soviet politics (Urban, 1994b, 1998, 2006) appear to stem from the eclipse of the political by the professional and its incommodious companion, morality. Not only is communication distorted by the fact that the same signifier – "professional" – is used to connote very different signifieds, but opposing codes induce mutual blame-laying against opponents. "Look what they claim to be doing here [as *I decode* their statements], and then look at what they have actually done." Yet as important as it may be to record the results of this eclipse of politics, it would be foolish either to hold culpable those who favor a moral interpretation of the political world or to exonerate those ostensibly employing a more politically nuanced discourse in which truth and morality are relative values. Relative to what? Were those in power to set up a collection of rules – however one-sided – and then, out of self-interest, proceed to violate those same rules with impunity, then there would be clear grounds for insisting on accountability and accusing power of illegal actions.[3] Those accusations would, in the end, draw on a moral discourse of fairness and, according both to Weber's concept of politics as well as to the model of political discourse advanced here, be nonetheless political for it. It may be that the actions of those in power are sufficiently reprehensible to demand moral censure, in which case one would be speaking the language of politics, too.

The second conclusion of import that can be drawn from this analysis concerns a return to a more recognizably political discourse after the hiatus of the El'tsin years. That is, the Gorbachev and Putin cohorts distinguish themselves from the other three groups in the sample by featuring in their narratives the discursive elements present in the right-hand column of Table 5.1, while the other groups more employ the elements listed in the left-hand column. On one hand, this return to political discourse signals a normalization that had been interrupted or suspended by the language of "reform" in the El'tsin years, and its attendant groups of professionals in politics who had framed their identities and roles as bringers of expert knowledge

---

[3] Examples of such practices in Russian politics are legion. For illustrations from the elections to the first Duma in 1993, see Urban (1994a); for illustrations from the presidential election of 1996, see Urban (1997).

and professional ethics to the affairs of state. This finding is consistent with Garcelon's notion of "interregnum" referenced in Chapter 1. Within the scope of their discourse, citizens appear simply as passive recipients of the presumed benefactions performed for them by professionals. On the other hand, however, citizens neither occupy a more prominent space nor are they accorded much agency in the narratives of either the Gorbachev or Putin cohorts. At most, they appear as constituents with whom politicians in the Putin era sometimes converse (*E4; E5*), or as an undifferentiated "people" whose welfare is the responsibility of the politician to protect (*E3*). To be sure, there are other aspects of the narratives of the Putin cohort that speak to political questions: a recognition of conflict as a normal feature of political life; the perception of ethics as situational; a tolerance for ambiguity such that one can continue to pursue goals in the face of resistance and disorder and to expect that those goals will be only imperfectly realized. Nonetheless, the tendency in their narratives to exclude mention of the citizenry and a public purpose toward which they strive would both support the notion of a weak sense of community and approval in Russian political discourse and reflect an incompleteness of the country's political transition in a practical sense.

This finding would call into question both the conceptualization and empirical results of much of the work on Russian political culture reported in the post-Soviet period.[4] Guided by the notion of "democratization," many scholars adopted the view that both elites and masses were learning a new political code and that they were in the process of internalizing democratic values. Richard Anderson (2001: 97), for example, whose work represents perhaps the most accomplished and astute version of this argument, has contended that democratization has consisted of "a new elite political discourse [that] converges on the ordinary language of the people formerly excluded from political activity ... [D]emocracy emerges when political discourse changes from linguistic cues that isolate the elite from

---

[4] For a summary of some of this work, see Fleron (1996).

the people to linguistic cues that merge the elite into the people."
Underlying this viewpoint seem to be two assumptions that distinguish it from the one that I have adopted here: namely, that the
political world is composed of pre-existing subjects who respond to
linguistic cues on the basis, in this case, of an ordinary language that
they already possess; and, secondly, that change in language usage has
proceeded as a linear process in the direction of democratization. In
contrast to the methodological individualism represented in the first
assumption, I have chosen a discourse-centered method whereby
subjects are constituted by the discourse(s) informing their "self"-
expression. On this tack, it becomes possible to distinguish the idea
of social subjects – those employing a given discourse – from that of
individuals said to possess certain beliefs, values or ideas.[5] As such, a
variety of subjects can be imagined, depending upon the variety of
discourses in circulation. This point, then, would undermine the
notion of linearity that has informed the bulk of studies on Russian
political culture in the transition period and open up the possibility of
another directionality for the process of change.

In an earlier study (Urban, 1996), I have advanced a cyclical
model of change in Russian political discourse that locates the
impetus for a discursive elaboration of "the new" in the thematization
of problems associated with "the old." Accordingly, the communicative blockages associated with doctrinaire communism were to be
removed by the discourse of *perestroika* that not only subverted the
old order but led to an intolerable discursive pluralism extinguished
for practical purposes by El'tsin's 1993 *coup d'état*. Thereafter, a search
was begun for a new, uniform, public discourse, an official ideology
that would return political life to a state resembling that which existed
prior to *perestroika* (Urban, 1998). The closing of this cycle seems to be
under way at present in the form of a new doctrine of "sovereign
democracy" advanced by the Putin regime. The cycle, itself, appears

[5] For a comparable approach applying discourse analysis to post-communist Poland
and Russia, see Kubik (2003).

to be reflected in the interview results reported here, which show a comparable discourse in use for the Gorbachev- and Putin-era cohorts that distinguishes them from the discursive structures employed by the other groups in the sample. To date, Russian political discourse may not have come full circle, back to the stifling uniformity and manifest absurdity of an all-embracing state ideology such as Marxism–Leninism. But that seems to be the direction, all the same.[6]

During the middle of the 2000s, the Putin administration began to formulate a systematic and comprehensive doctrine of state by detaching words from their common meanings and shoe-horning them into categories where they might ordinarily not belong. The doctrine borne of their efforts, "sovereign democracy," is said to represent an answer to the principal problem confronting Russia: *viz.*, "how to be part of the human commonweal and simultaneously preserve the freedom of one's own self-determination" (Polyakov, 2007: 4). The rub, it would seem, is that this commonweal has been dominated by foreign powers, their associated international financial institutions and transnational corporations that endlessly think of new and more clever ways to exploit Russia. In the words of the doctrine's principal architect, Vladislav Surkov:

> all they would seem to want for us to be would be a security
> service to protect the pipelines running through our territory.
> But this means that they are competitors, not enemies. That's how
> businessmen think. Nothing personal. They just take everything up
> to the last boot, in a politically correct way and with all respect. This
> is normal. We must relate to it calmly . . . and become competitive
> *(Surkov, 2007: 48).*

Sovereignty, then, hinges on the state's ability to foster a *national* bourgeoisie – in place of the "off-shore aristocracy" (Surkov, 2007: 55)

---

[6] The new state doctrine of "sovereign democracy" is addressed by a number of officials and commentators on public affairs in Garadzha (2006) and Pavlovskii (2007).

that flourished in the El'tsin years – that will make Russia again a competitor in world affairs. And democracy? It is the alleged product of the adjective "sovereign," representing a "geopolitical synonym for the freedom of the people" (Polyakov, 2007: 4–5). The doctrine draws its warrant by referencing a long line of personages and institutions – from tsarist times till the present – said to have saved, bolstered and modernized Russia's sovereignty. Yet nowhere is there mention of any public.[7] The community appears only as a collection of opinion polls on Putin's popularity and as the would-be beneficiaries of state action. For its part, law seems confined to the status of the executive's injunction: "Fulfill that which is written here in the Constitution. Such-and-such is written there. Fulfill it" (Surkov, 2007: 43). Sovereign democracy thus dispenses with political equality by explicitly distinguishing a class of officialdom and businessmen who run things for the alleged benefit of everyone else. In so doing, it eclipses the dimensions of political discourse predicated on equality – community and approval – and thus both conforms to and reproduces Russia's specific variant of a political discourse that relies on the personally oriented categories of competence and morality. Its subtext – that the state is governed by competent people committed to enhancing the country's sovereignty and, thereby, the welfare of the population – appears to be apposite to the forms of personalized relations characteristic of Civil Society *II*. Those forms are here appropriated and reworked by officialdom to construct an identity and a project around the empty signifier of "sovereign democracy," itself a justification for hierarchy and their respective positions within it. Democracy is what they do, incongruously, because they are the ones who are competent and moral.

---

[7] In a recent volume, over a dozen essays by both Russian and Western observers – most of which employ Laclau's Discourse Theory (in which "the people" is framed as the central category in modern political speech) – analyze Putin-era discourse in general and "sovereign democracy" in particular. None reports even a trace of a popular presence in the language of the current regime. See the many essays on these subjects in Casula and Perovic (2009).

Traces of this doctrine appear in the discourse exhibited by the Putin group in this study. Their remarks evince a political managerialism whose subjects have developed exclusionary codes structuring their communication on public matters. There seems to be little, if any, room for the citizenry in their narratives. For instance, although four of the five Putin-era respondents are members of the State Duma, not one interpreted the question about personal relations in politics as having anything to do with constituents. Thus, while some elements of the political are more apparent in their narratives than they are in those of the other four cohorts in the sample, these narratives nonetheless record the distance in Russian political life separating state from society.

6   Revolution

We were all participants in a broad liberation movement ... a new humanism for the twenty-first century (B4).

It's a well-known formula: romantics make revolutions and their fruits are appropriated by completely different people (D3).

Gorbachev tried honesty and probity. Gorbachev tried. And what was the result? El'tsin handed over the country to the devil's mother (A4).

Between Gorbachev's *perestroika* and the Belovezh Accords that sundered the USSR, Russia experienced a political revolution. The new state almost immediately instituted a set of policies that extended this revolution to economy and society, transforming the country in a few years in ways scarcely imaginable less than a decade earlier. This chapter focuses on the characterizations of those events reflected in the consciousness of the country's political class roughly a decade later. How do they recall this revolution? What features has it acquired (or shed) with respect to situating in memory its foundational significance for a young country born of an old civilization and culture?

Interestingly, although the interview prompts did not include the term "revolution," some twenty respondents nonetheless used that word in one way or another to describe the events just mentioned. In a number of instances, it popped up in their replies to the final question that they were asked concerning their relations then and now to the events of August 1991 (the failed Soviet *coup d'état* and the resistance to it) and the Belovezh Accords concluded in the following December.[1] But subjects also introduced the term

---

[1] The final item in that prompt, which concerns the events of autumn 1999, the period of Putin's rise to power, attracted surprisingly little comment and is, therefore, not included here.

themselves while commenting on a variety of other topics. It is, of course, worth recalling that the interview sample on which this study is based by no means includes all of the forces contending on Russia's political field. Rather, it consists of those who in one way or another supported the general ideas informing the revolution, if not always the specific forms that it eventually took. Indeed, the overwhelming majority of respondents had been participants in the revolution itself, whether on the barricades, the floors of meeting halls and legislatures, or the corridors of state power. Their remembrances and retrospective characterizations vary considerably, often in categorical disagreement with one another. In many cases, their assessments of seminal events cluster around the cognitive networks with which they have been associated. But not always.

The interview narratives evince enough dissension on fundamental issues related to Russia's recent revolution to discourage any interpretive effort based on first facts. Respondents simply do not agree on: (1) when the revolution began; (2) when it ended; (3) what it was about; (4) whether, and to what extent, its objectives were met; and (5) what it has meant for the country's future. Moreover, its key dimensions – political liberation and socioeconomic transformation – are so bitterly contested in their accounts that it would seem that there is no harmonious, much less singular, collection of memories within the political class constituting this revolution as a specific set of acknowledged events. For that class itself, it would seem, there is not one revolution but several.[2]

A counterfactual deserves mention in this respect; namely, the absence of any national commemoration of Russia's late revolution. That absence would seem to have great signicance for the founding of a new state, connoting an ellipsis in the collective life of the nation, its identity and its sense of time and space (Connerton, 1989). To be sure,

---

[2] The extreme case here would be represented by one respondent (A2) who reversed a conception common to others that the revolution was initiated in the *perestroika* period. In his view, *perestroika* was an attempt to call off the continuing Revolution of 1917 in order to reach a compromise with society.

there were gatherings and a rock concert to celebrate the first anniversary of the defeat of the August coup, just as another rock concert was staged in Moscow on the tenth anniversary of that event. Otherwise – and despite some official efforts to promote commemoration (Smith, 2002: Urban, 1998) – there has been effectively nothing, and this in a country in which remembrance of things past represents a highly honored tradition (Clark, 1995). How to account for dissension among those in the political class on the issue of what happened, and for the blank spot in society's collective remembrance of the revolution?

I approach these two issues by taking the individual dimensions of Russian political discourse, discussed separately in the preceding chapters, and applying them in concert to the interview narratives. In so doing, I wish to show how their particular configuration in the discourse – discussed to this point somewhat thematically – functions as a whole to generate various narrative programs addressed to the specific topic of revolution. As demonstrated above, the dimensions of morality and competence are salient while those of community and approval are either muted or absent altogether. This condition, I intend to show here, militates against common conceptions and leads to rigid position-taking among participants. Position-taking, in turn, is structured by two binaries derived from the two active elements in the discourse: fate/agency, which is derived from "competence"; and romance/anti-romance, which issues from "morality." Respondents weave the elements and the binaries together in complex ways that establish the various positions that they take on the field of political communication.

In order to illustrate this process, consider the five examples set out in Table 6.1. Each is bordered on the left-hand margin by abbreviations for the two relevant discourse elements, represented either in the positive (competent, moral) or the negative (incompetent, immoral), followed by the binary structures (fate/agency and romance/anti-romance) active in the respective statements that follow. The statements themselves are paraphrases of numerous comments made by subjects on the topic of revolution. They

Table 6.1 *Five permutations of discourse elements and binary structures in narratives on revolution*

Discourse elements: *C* = Competence (positive and negative).
M = Morality (positive and negative).

1. *C* +, *M* +, *a, ro* We, the revolutionaries, were able to recognize the real situation and to take actions that prevented catastrophe.
2. *C* +, *M* +, *f* Although we did what was needed to be done, the revolutionary situation in which we acted involved unforeseeable consequences.
3. *C* −, *M* +, *a, ar* We were motivated by the highest ideals but didn't appreciate that others would use the opportunities that we created to enrich themselves.
4. *C* −, *a* They acted out of ignorance and this led to calamity.
5. *M* −, *a, ar* Their greed for power and money led the country to ruin.

represent effectively all positions on this topic taken by members of the sample.

The first row in Table 6.1 contains a statement that combines competence and morality. The speaker claims the ability to have recognized what needed to be done, to have done it, and thereby to have achieved a beneficial result. It also activates both sides of the fate/agency binary by implying a set of objective circumstances (fate) which has been recognized and dealt with (agency). Finally, the element of romance is contained in the reference to extraordinary people, revolutionaries, steering things toward a happy ending. In the second statement, however, competence and morality are combined in a different fashion, owing to the way in which fate is deployed: a "revolutionary situation" producing consequences that are negatively marked but which absolve the speaker of agency causing immorality. The third statement invokes agency and romance – "motivated by the highest ideals" – but introduces competence or, more precisely, its lack, as exculpation for moral consequences. This pairing of morality and (in)competence yields anti-romance, a category conditioned by the implicit presence of a villain ("others") acting immorally. The fourth statement is accusatory, affixing responsibility by reference to agency (it happened because they did it) while simultaneously impugning the competence of the agents. The final statement is constructed by affirming agency – but not necessarily competence – and by denying morality, thus summoning the category "anti-romance."

As varied and opposed as these statements appear to be, it should be emphasized that they all partake of a single political discourse. That is, each statement is constructed from out of the same collection of root terms, even while it might reverse the valence of those terms and combine them in ways that differ from those present in other assertions. Taken together, the elementary terms, when activated in specific narratives, yield a single field of political communication on which speakers take their respective positions. The following section examines the discursive strategies of the subjects yielding those positions on the topic of political revolution, while the one that succeeds it repeats that examination with a focus on the ensuing socioeconomic transformation.

THE EMERGENCE OF THE RUSSIAN STATE

A sizeable contingent of respondents used notions of things objective and inevitable to account for Russia's revolution, thus invoking the fate/agency binary by underscoring its first term. One responded to what he anticipated to be my objection to his comment that the collapse of the Soviet Union transpired "objectively" by retorting that

> No, this is not difficult [to understand] it is absolutely [the case]. The Union was absolutely doomed ... As soon as the clamps were weakened. Either there would be a totalitarian regime or none whatsoever. There was no middle ground. As soon as fear disappears, freedom arises (B6).

Another responded that:

> The USSR was objectively unmanageable: it was too large a country, with too many nations [in it], too many religions, too

much of all that might have a chance to exist as a unified whole
only with a totalitarian regime [holding it together] (A1).

Similarly, a third remarked that, concerning the collapse of the USSR,
he saw "the centrifugal forces as, well, absolutely inescapable ... as
an expected inevitability" (B3).

In distinction from the mechanistic metaphors informing these
remarks – all three of which reference some mechanism no longer
able to hold the parts together – a fourth respondent used a biological
one. Referring to how the defeat of the 1991 August putsch led
directly to the extinction of the USSR, he commented that:

> the putsch showed that our society had an incurable disease.
> Politically it was a Chernobyl – that is, radiation that
> penetrated the brain, the will and all the pores of the social
> organism. Therefore, the August events helped me to work out
> the concept of political radiation. The ways in which state,
> society and the life of the individual are organized ... represent
> their particular fate. [Political] radiation is continuously needed
> to heal it (B4).

Along with these characterizations, five other individuals in
the sample attributed the collapse of the USSR, and thus the origins
of the contemporary Russian state, to inescapable, impersonal and
objective factors (B9, B10, C3, E2 and E5), although two of them
thought it nonetheless a tragedy (B9, E5). Others, apparently more
positively disposed toward the USSR's extinction, introduced a
human element into their assessments. One cited Vladimir Putin's
characterization that the USSR's end amounted to a "civilized
divorce" (E1). Another similarly maintained that in the face of the
fact that "all of the [union] republics were scattering and unprepared
to sign [a new treaty on the union], this was the practically moral
thing to do" (B5). Two others introduced the counterfactual of
violence and bloodshed (B8 and C5). As one put it:

> I think that a responsible decision was taken. If you ask yourself
> why did the train of events in the Soviet Union and Yugoslavia

proceed along different tracks, why in Yugoslavia there was bloody porridge and on the post-Soviet expanse there were many unpleasant things but nothing like that, and if you want an answer in one sentence, then I will tell you that it was because we signed the Belovezh Accords (*B*8).

In sharp contrast to these characterizations, some thirteen members of the sample took the position that human hand lay behind the USSR's disintegration and evaluated that event negatively. In this respect, the five contingents of respondents map very closely onto the positions taken regarding this event. As expected, those from the first and second El'tsin administrations – two of whom participated directly in signing the Belovezh Accords – were most favorably inclined toward the result. Two from those groups did register their disapproval of what had occurred, but they were peripheral members of these cohorts (*B*1, *C*4). Those outside the two El'tsin groups, however, took very strong exception. The harshest remonstrations from members of these groups labeled Russia's signators to the Belovezh Accords "criminals" (*E*4) and "traitors."

- It was treason, treason for the sake of power. They got together, drank champagne and [someone said] "I'll telephone [then US president] Bush." Understand? You know how gratifying is self-esteem – "Here we are the ones who have torn down the Soviet Union!" Even Bush himself was surprised (*A*4).
- In the final analysis, it was a crime. At the time I wasn't a harsh critic, and all the same I then couldn't have been because I was on El'tsin's side or because I was insufficiently aware that this was the destruction of the country and such a tragedy for the Russians who remained beyond our borders. It was an adventure ending in a huge tragedy for many, many millions of people (*D*2).
- In November [1991] I was conversing with [Nursultan] Nazarbaev [president of Kazakhstan – M. U.]. He told me that there were chances to preserve the USSR, but El'tsin was categorically opposed to it. He [El'tsin] wanted the Kremlin, not the country, and was absolutely

uninterested in legitimacy, in democracy. And the Belovezh
Accords were ratified not only by the liberal-democrats but by the
communists. There was not a single party here which stood for right
and for law (A5).

These remarks – underscoring treason and criminality – invert the
terms of competence and morality while emphasizing the element
of agency. According to their subtext, evil people get together to
perpetrate evil. The inversion of competence and morality is particularly pronounced in the first statement where the phrase,
"drank champagne," simultaneously signifies both a celebration
of evil-doing and – because it obliquely references broad background understandings in Russia that the principal signators of
the Accords were at the time inebriated – an outright surrender of
mental faculties.

Respondents rarely drew on a discourse of community to
address the matter of a Russian state emerging from the ruins of the
USSR. When they did, it was coupled with that of morality. However,
just whom the community included and what moral purpose was
served were subject to contention. This was true even for those in the
same cohort, as in the case of two members of Yabloko who linked
community and morality – here signified by "democracy" – in
opposing ways. One said that he had

> voted for the Belovezh Accords in the Supreme Soviet, but
> overall that was a mistake because the collapse of the USSR
> was for me a political and personal tragedy. I should have
> abstained. But reflecting on it over and over I think that what
> happened was unavoidable ... We couldn't hold on to the Baltic
> states and Georgia without shedding a lot of blood. But we
> probably could have held on to Central Asia. But the course
> of my thoughts has led me to recognize the regimes
> remaining there, such as Turkmenbashi [then president of
> Turkmenistan – M. U.] ... Well, what if Turkmenistan had
> remained in Russia? He would have installed the same regime

there that exists today and would have exerted colossal pressure on Moscow, on the central authorities. So I think that maybe it was better that these [Central Asian] republics were pulled away from us (D7).

One of his colleagues took just the opposite approach to the issue of democracy and community, arguing that he had wanted

all of the Soviet Union to become a democratic country ...
I thought that Russia, which had dragged all the others into communism, bore responsibility for gradually building democracy in the entire country. That's all there is to it ... The economic treaty creating a single market for a new union had already been signed and it was destroyed in the Belovezh woods. I knew that that would lead to very big difficulties but, more, I wanted the whole country to become democratic (D6).

Alongside these remarks about community in the abstract – Whom might it or should it include? – numerous subjects underscore the sad consequences for communities in the flesh: families now divided by state borders; Russian populations in other of the former union republics who would face discrimination and worse. Yet whether referring to the abstract or the concrete, all references to community in the context of the USSR's breakup frame "community" in passive terms. Consistent with the discussion in Chapter 3, "community" functions in Russian political discourse as the recipient of benefits bestowed by the political class – as references to the prevention of bloodletting, above, would indicate – or as an impoverished, neglected or abused entity supplying political actors with reason to blame others for criminal or traitorous deeds. Yet "community" itself displays no agency in these narratives. No respondent remarked on what the people did: what they approved, what they wanted, what they opposed. Of course, what they did may have been little or nothing at all. The point, however, is that within the discourse they do not seem to be expected to do anything.

Finally, with respect to the disintegration of the USSR, a discourse of competence was employed by a few respondents who grafted it onto those of morality and community. Some – especially two in the sample who participated directly in the meeting where the Accords were concluded – categorically insisted that the statecraft displayed at Belovezh rescued Russia from an otherwise sanguinary fate. Others, however, took the opposite view. For instance, the comments of A5 about right and law, above, suggest a failure on the part of all political forces to apprehend a decisive political moment and to act accordingly. Another respondent recalled that as advisor to a four-member fraction of deputies in the Supreme Soviet, he had persuaded them to join two others to vote against the Accords, thus implying that the vast majority of Russia's legislators did not display the competence to check "collusion at the top" or consider the real consequences of their actions (C4). A third respondent argued that the demise of the USSR could have been at least delayed for a very long time were the political class capable of recognizing realities (D1), while a fourth remarked that once in power in the Russian Republic, the El'tsin administration was witness to

> the appointment of extremely incompetent, utterly unthinking people to the most important posts. Their behavior during the August putsch had already made this clear to me. Of course, they achieved victory then, but a victory over an absolutely incapable opponent which got them accustomed to thinking that everything is just that easy. They were not prepared to deal with the country's real problems. And so, when it came to the Belovezh Accords, they wanted just to get something done as quickly as possible, not thinking of the cost or consequences, just, "Hurrah! We've solved the major problems." They lost their own country and no one thought about that (D4).

Given the enormity of the events in question and whether or not respondents participated in them, it is not surprising that the narratives occasioned by the prompt to assess the Belovezh Accords are as polarized as they are. However, some fifteen years after the fact, respondents resort almost exclusively to strong signifiers – whether, on one hand, praising the principals for saving the country from a blood bath or, on the other, condemning them as criminals and traitors – which indicate the semiotic load borne by the moral dimension of Russian political discourse. The same appears to be true for the category, competence. The principals in this case are described as either masters of statecraft or as irresponsible, "utterly unthinking" people. Thus, it is not merely the division obtaining among respondents with respect to this issue but its depth that invites comment. It would seem that the unbridgeable divide evinced here is contingent upon the relative absence of a recognized community, and, consequently, upon speakers' ability to reference a discourse of approval. In that absence, subjects construct themselves on the issue of the origin of their state by using the categories available to them: morality and competence. In so doing, they draw black-and-white distinctions: either statesmen acting on moral grounds achieved an optimal result by terminating the existence of the Soviet Union, or fools with no sense of moral responsibility perpetrated a treacherous crime. Thus, in the origins of their state, Russia's political class appears to be sharply divided into exponents of approbation and opprobrium.

SOCIOECONOMIC TRANSFORMATION

In the same way that narratives of approbation and opprobrium regarding the origins of the Russian state are informed by discourses of morality and competence, so respondents drawing on these same discourses to address the matter of Russia's ensuing socioeconomic transformation divide themselves into two opposing groups: some argue that the rapid installation of capitalism represented an optimal response to objective circumstances, thus rescuing the country from great misfortune; others claim that the actual measures carried out were misguided, amateurish and, for some, larcenous, thus pitching the country into calamity. Here, the binary of fate/agency underpinning narratives regarding the USSR's termination appears again in the interview texts. In commenting on the country's internal transformation, the second binary – romance/anti-romance – also surfaces. Both binaries, however, allow for considerable variation in the way in which signifiers are deployed.

To illustrate, take for example the use of the word "Bolshevik." This word had been a seminal marker in the discourse of the Soviet regime, a pivotal part of the master tale that it propagated in all media, identifying citizens according to their receptivity to, and facility with, retelling the tale of proletarian revolution, the vanquishing of class enemies, the inauguration of the first socialist state, and so on (Bourmeyster, 1983). Within the confines of Soviet discourse, "Bolshevik" conveyed the romance of the regime's version of the 1917 Revolution. It stood for only the most admirable qualities – selflessness, unswerving dedication, intellectual brilliance and unshakeable courage – placed in service to the cause of all humanity. During the country's more recent revolution, however, this same term's valence was reversed by anti-communist forces who used it as verbal artillery in their assault on the Soviet party-state. In their discourse, "Bolshevik" was associated with adjectives such as "dogmatic," "ruthless," "mendacious" and "murderous," thus impugning the foundational myths of the order that they sought to overthrow. Although "Bolshevik" was seldom used by respondents in the present study, its appearance in the narratives of two of them indicates how specific terms can take on a penumbra of meaning and thus function as empty signifiers, in this instance, both negatively and ironically. One member of the sample – himself a former career official in the Communist Party of the Soviet Union with Politburo rank – castigated the "democrats" who had come to power in communism's wake as "barbarous" and "lawless" hotheads who had betrayed democracy itself. He thus named them "Bolsheviks, but inside-out" (A4). A member of that same government excoriated by this respondent, appropriated the very same term, "Bolsheviks," for himself and his colleagues, thus ironically returning the word's meaning to something like the one that it had had in Soviet times (B9).[3]

Mindful of this possibility for signifiers "to float" – that is, to be used simultaneously by those on contending sides of a political conflict who supply them with different, even opposing, meanings (Laclau, 2005), I would like to review the interview narratives addressed to the social and economic aspects of Russia's anti-communist revolution, situating signifiers within the structure of the discourses in which they appear. In so doing, my purpose is twofold: (1) to distinguish analytically those signifiers anchored in the agency/fate binary from those based on the couple, romance/anti-romance; and (2) to disentangle the intertwined discourses of morality, competence and community reflected in the interview narratives. Consistent with that approach, my aim is to locate those root discursive categories through which political actors articulate their sense of the world and their roles within it.

The fate/agency binary. The interview narratives – as the example above concerning the usage of the term "Bolshevik" might suggest – in many instances evince a blurring of significance, a crossing of semantic boundaries, even a reversal of meanings. The notions of agency, as subjects producing results, and fate, as objective conditions impervious to human device, are in like manner both opposed and conjoined in respondents' remarks, producing certain permutations and qualifications on the surface level of narrative that resist interpretation in the absence of their discursive context. With that in mind, I shall review the relevance of these structuring terms by taking first their more straightforward expressions in respondents' narratives, moving then to the more complex ways in which they were used. I begin with "fate."

The most direct expression of the category "fate" in respondents' statements took the form of "no alternative." This mode of

---

[3] To extend the (positive) analogy, this respondent used the term employed by the Bolsheviks for members of the government apparatus that they inherited – i.e., "bourgeois specialists" – to refer to Soviet officialdom that he was obliged to direct once having entered the government.

characterization had been employed during *perestroika*, and was used by both Gorbachev (1987) and members of the liberal intelligentsia (Afanas'ev, 1988) as a basis for advancing radical solutions to problems regarded as endemic to the Soviet system. Some twenty years later, this same notion of inescapable objectivity surfaced in the narratives of a few interview subjects who remarked that

- We [in the government instituting the economic reforms] did that which we considered to be absolutely necessary, and perhaps there simply were not any alternatives to the decisions that we took. But it is necessary to understand that many of the decisions that you take can later be used against you by others (B9).
- I think that as a matter of fact there were no alternatives to that group [of reformers], which is why they came to power (B7).
- I was leading the government and I had to secure things so that we [the country] could last until [the next] harvest and thus would not have to endure a famine like the one that occurred in 1918 (B8).

The third set of remarks above displays in concentrated form the associations made in interview narratives among fate, agency, morality and competence. Here, grasping the objective situation implies the competence to recognize fate, while activating that consciousness by means of beneficial policy measures secures the moral outcome of rescuing the country from famine. This same subject connected these categories in another respect remarking that:

> In November 1991, when the condition of the Soviet economy was absolutely catastrophic, I was invited to head up de facto the economics sector in the Russian government. We had prepared a satisfactorily comprehensive plan of action for what needed to be done in order to conduct reanimating measures to rebuild [the economy] from its ruins (B8).

Here, the metaphors of reanimation and ruins convey the notion of objective conditions associated with fate, while preparing a "comprehensive plan of action" speaks to the issues of agency and competence.

These metaphors appear not infrequently in the comments of members of the team of economists setting policy in the first El'tsin administration, just as they do among those of others in both El'tsin-era cohorts. However, outside of the economic reform team itself, evaluations of agency could differ even while the context would be objectified by the trope "reanimation." As one respondent from the second El'tsin administration remarked in reference to the team of reformers:

> Imagine the following situation: they were trying to revive a sick man but as a matter of fact this person was already clinically dead. So here we are not talking about a program that might make a healthy human being more healthy; rather, we are talking about how to bring an organism back to life. So, they administered adrenaline to the heart, gave a massage, administered electric shock. It might be possible to call such measures a program, but these were actually emergency measures to restore an organism to life ... They didn't have any kind of detailed program that they had worked out (C3).

Noteworthy here would be the fact that this interview subject uses the very language of fate and agency – reanimation of a corpse by means of shock therapy – that the reform team employs to describe their situation and actions. However, while sharing in their metaphoric construction of conditions facing the government at the time, C3 also subtracts from their actions a large measure of competence. In this respect, his assessment appears to shade into that of many in other cohorts who lambaste the team of reformers for ineptitude. Yet his narrative dovetails with that of the reformers in their common recognition of fate, a recognition supplied by the substitution of a medical metaphor for economic terms, proper (Verdery, 1996). Respondents who did not participate in that metaphoric construction thus took a far dimmer view of this team and their actions, producing accusatory narratives drawing on the discourses of morality as well as competence.

With respect to the discourse of competence, perhaps the most blistering and sustained critique was submitted by one interview subject who had himself been a somewhat peripheral member of the reform team. His words are worth quoting at length.

> I don't know what to say about my time in the Gaidar government. In principle, I had good relations with Gaidar, but that period in government was the most unpleasant in my life . . . I had a background in bankruptcy – which was essentially what privatization was about in my country. I had lived and worked in the USA. Therefore, I noticed in the Gaidar government a deficit of knowledge. A big role in the formation of that government was played by a study group [*kruzhok*] in economics that began meeting toward the end of the 1980s. I was not a participant. But when the reforms were conducted, the experiences from that group proved more important than those of actual, living people. They perceived market relations and private property to be the solution to all problems. They were excessively naïve . . . In 1990, Jeffrey Sachs appeared in Moscow and so did the firm, Goldman Sachs. I had to explain to a whole bunch of well-known political actors that they were not half-brothers as some of them had thought. The level of understanding of capitalism was completely nil. All their knowledge had come from [Soviet] textbooks. They had never lived under capitalism as I had, nor at that time could most of those instituting the reforms read English well enough to comprehend complex economic texts. No one had a Western education. This had a very strong effect on things (*B*1).[4]

---

[4] Facility with the English language seems to play no small role in assessments of competence among some in the sample, perhaps signifying one's place in the world order – and here terms such as the "civilized" or the "normal" countries are used as markers of association with the West – that seems to matter greatly in contemporary Russian culture (Boym, 2001: Lemon, 2000). Thus, whereas *B*1 reports in his criticism of others on the reform team their deficit of skills in that tongue, *B*9 insists that: "I remember the first discussions in Europe with the International Monetary Fund. We conducted them in English. Well, because there are always translators, this is not so important. But I speak about it [to indicate] the level of education among those who were then in power" (*B*9). The accuracy of these conflicting assessments is in the present context far less significant than is the fact that this form of cultural capital – ability in the English language – occupies such a prominent place in the outlook of the economic reform team.

This assessment of the competence of the reformers in government was shared by members of the Yabloko contingent in the sample. But, as discussed in Chapter 4, their narratives reflected in almost equal measure a discourse of morality impugning the results of, if not always the intentions behind, the actions of the reformers. Putin-era respondents, on the other hand, said very little about these things, except to castigate the reformers for weakening the Russian state and for doing the bidding of foreign powers (E3, E4). Interestingly, those in the Gorbachev-era cohort in this instance most resembled the Yabloko group in their assessments, employing the discourses of competence and morality. Here is a sample of their remarks:

- The mistake [of the reformers] was both to neglect Russia's history and to think up anything new. They just took the European code as a cultural-political model to follow. As they understood it, it meant a return to private property, a redistribution of basic resources, of the productive bases of the country's own might. To place those resources in private hands. But the important political question was: *Into whose hands?* How do they decide what to do with them? To buy [the British football club] Chelsea?[5] To build dachas in Nice? To purchase yachts? But the use of these resources should have not been for the sake of a few to live better, but to modernize the country, to replace its technology ... I think that our economic reformers [believed in] this mythology: If property belongs to private individuals, everything automatically goes well. They simply didn't know that property is not a thing but a system of relations (A2).
- What kind of principles did the El'tsin group display? None. "You get the oil and I'll take the gas," that's all. But the question arises: To what purpose will the oil be put? For the national interest or for Abramovich[6] to buy a yacht? ... Shock therapy and privatization were

---

[5] The reference to the Chelsea Football Club concerns its scandalous purchase by a Russian, Roman Abramovich, who profited greatly from the reforms.

[6] Abramovich is the same individual referred to in the previous note.

carried out immorally, not to build democracy or a market but just to enrich certain people or those close to them (A4).

• In my view, there was no need whatsoever to change the governing class [*nomenklatura*]. They were already de-ideologized. They were capable of administering the country . . . But the tragedy was that under the banner of democracy, real Bolsheviks came to power for whom power and money were more important than any democracy. Out of this came the shelling of the White House[7] and the end of Russian democracy. And now those same people complain about Putin. But there's no difference, absolutely none. The current system was formed when they adopted the 1993 Constitution, actually, an elected autocracy. You can't blame Putin for that! Recently I asked Irina Khakamada[8] about this and she said, "Sasha, you're right." Her liberals created this system for themselves, not thinking that it could ever be [put to use] by their opponents (A5).[9]

Romance/anti-romance. The last of the remarks just quoted touches on the binary "romance/anti-romance." It subverts a celebratory moment in the narratives of reformers in an "anti-romantic" way by implicating them in the demise of the very value, democracy, that they have claimed to promote. Others – both reformers and some of their critics – often endow their narratives with direct mention of "romance," lacing them in many instances with references to the heady atmosphere of the period in which they acted, conjuring and

---

[7] This reference is to El'tsin's 1993 *coup d'état* and the military assault on the opposition legislature, then ensconced in a building called the "White House" by Russians.

[8] At the time, Irina Khakamada was a leader of the Union of Right Forces, something of a political successor to that wing of the reform movement represented earlier in the Gaidar government.

[9] A member of the first El'tsin administration – who, as a longtime dissident in the Soviet period, belonged to a cognitive network quite different from that of the economic reformers – similarly remarked that "the transition from El'tsin to Putin was a natural regularity that began with the events of 1993 and 1996 [El'tsin's coup and subsequent re-election – M. U.]. The first democrats had already decided that everything was permissible, that they could use any instruments if only democracy would remain in power. In the final analysis, they played a cruel joke on themselves" (B2).

speaking directly about a "romantic time," a "revolutionary time" (*C2*). In this respect, "romance" admits to two very different interpretations among members of the sample. In some instances, it is marked positively. Comparing it to the 2004–2005 mass political protests in Ukraine that brought down an illegitimate government, one respondent referred to the defeat of the August 1991 Soviet putsch as "our Orange Revolution" (*E1*). Another recalled that:

> Those three days and nights (19–21 August 1991 – M. U.) were some of the brightest in my life. I was at the White House day and night.[10] When I got news of the putsch, all that I had been hoping for seemed dashed. But when I saw my comrades, when I saw that we would resist and not give in, all my perplexity and bitterness passed. I understood that I was in a circle of people who would not lie down before what had happened ... It was resistance that put me in a wonderful frame of mind (*D7*).

The defeat of the Soviet putsch represents for many in the sample the ground zero of Russia's revolution. Issuing from those events, the statehood of the country was secured and its social and economic transformation was made possible. Both appear in the narratives of those in the first El'tsin administration as seamlessly connected. In the words of one:

> In my own life I always perceived how difficult and torturous is the attempt to move the country from empire to freedom. Of course, I am immeasurably glad that in 1990, 1991 and 1992 I had a decisive influence on working out the principal ideas connected with reform, modernization and the transformation to a new Russia ... We were all participants in a broad liberation movement, each in his own, irreplicable way. In the Greek *polis*, politics was perceived as the highest, most rewarding, most prestigious and

---

[10] At this time, the White House was the seat of the Russian government and central locus of the resistance to the Soviet putsch.

significant activity, in equal measure securing personal honor, personal dignity and serving the common good. I have no doubt that such an elevated sense of politics was inside us in the nineties ... I still insist that the lessons of 1991 and Russia's contemporary possibilities enable the country to perform as, let's say, the active cultivator of a new humanism for the twenty-first century (B4).

Another respondent from the first El'tsin administration recalled how, in his field of foreign policy, revolutionary ideas brought himself and his colleague into conflict with all practitioners of conventional diplomacy, including his own superiors:

I served as deputy to Sergei Kovalev, the former dissident who then directed the Human Rights Committee in the Duma and headed the Russian delegation to the International Commission on Human Rights. The most surprising thing for us in Geneva, the most startling thing, was that the old Soviet diplomats behaved exactly like the Americans, the English, the European Commission and so forth. We understood it – this was a single family who, of course, had their own nook, their own interests and their own rules for defending them ... The adopting of resolutions was just buying and selling. Absolutely so. "You support me on this and I'll back you on that." But we were the revolutionaries of 1991 from the new Russia! We decided to knock all of that down. Naturally, this brought us into conflict with our own superiors whose arguments were absolutely understandable. They would say, for example, that "we have a 4,000-kilometer border with China. That's our neighbor, an influential, developing force" and so on. "We can't take [human rights] actions against them. That's not in the interest of the state." We would reply, "Why must we lie and defend them? Aren't we here for the purpose of *human rights*? On economic matters, please, go ahead and cooperate with them. But if the question concerns human rights, then we're just not going to neglect it." So, we argued with them, and never stopped (B2).

The impasse suffered by revolutionary ideals in confrontation with hardened political realities was even more poignantly referenced by others in the sample. Wistfully, two of them summed up their experience with revolution and romance in these words:

- Like many others in politics in those days [the late 1980s and early 1990s], I was an idealist. While idealists built castles in the air, pragmatists privatized the present. It's a well-known formula: romantics make revolutions and their fruits are appropriated by completely different people (D3).

- In August 1991, I was with El'tsin's team in the White House from the first. I was morally prepared to give my life defending democracy, the principles of freedom and justice, from the totalitarian, perverse order that previously for some reason had been calling itself "communist." Now, like many of my colleagues who then participated in this, I am deeply disappointed. We expected something else. Maybe we had something of a romantic view of things that would occur after our victory. But that didn't happen. Those who came to power did not, in my view, have to conduct reforms that impoverished a large part of the population or conduct privatization that gave over natural monopolies to private hands (D5).

These remarks invoke anti-romance, the idea that some force has devalued the actions that individuals had taken on behalf of ideals that, at least previously, had been quite real to them. Anti-romance in this respect represents disillusion, the act of shedding what turned out to be false hope. This notion informs a rather standard narrative in Russian politics employed by those liberal-democrats who had gone into opposition to their opposite numbers in government, imprecating them for etiolating, if not destroying, the values of liberal democracy to which both groups lay claim. Indeed, similar remarks on that score are sprinkled throughout the preceding pages of this study. Liberals in government – as if in reply to these charges – offered a diverse array of comments in their defense, although they were never directly queried about such matters, thus suggesting that a narrative of apology is every bit as much an element in the country's political discourse as is that of accusation. One tack taken by the reformers reverses the valence of *B1*'s remarks, quoted above, concerning the incestuous intellectual climate in the reform team that insulated its members from the world of practice and from the actual consequences of their actions. Rather than inbred thinking, two respondents proudly described their "team" as composed of *edinomyshlennikov* (*B8*, *B9*), a term that translates into English as "like-minded thinkers" but in Russian carries an even stronger sense of conformity, literally meaning something like "those of a single mind." In this usage, single-mindedness does not represent some fatal lack of sensitivity to things but – much like the signifier "Bolshevik" when deployed positively – a rare competence in service to morality.[11] Thus, between criticism and apology, there is no debate on this score. Those in the reform team all thought alike. Difference occurs only at the level of evaluation as to whether this was a good thing or not.

A second line of defense is set up by constructing "revolution" as a liminal time, a period in which people have been dislodged from the ordinary and thus a portal through which outsiders could enter politics (Horvath and Thomassen, 2008).

- Unconditionally, only in a romantic and revolutionary period could people such as myself get involved with high-level politics, as boys ready for battle who could pull the caftans from the fire. That's when El'tsin's circle got the idea to create a government out of proven fighters. [At first] we said, "Many thanks, but we can't bear responsibility and do anything serious in a government full of people without a program." So, for a long time – well not actually long, just a few days, for then time was flowing fast and slowly simultaneously – there was no government at all (*B9*).

---

[11] In the memoirs of this team's leader, the close relations within the team, along with their purported competence and morality, are rehearsed at some length (Gaidar, 1999).

- The old regime fell against the backdrop of new [Russian] institutions
  that were still weak. These, as it were, were revolutionary times.
  Again, I'll emphasize what I've said many times, that I don't
  understand there to be anything romantic about a revolution.
  In general, a revolution is a horrible tragedy for any society, the
  consequence of a regime unable to solve those problems that might
  have been settled earlier in an altogether different way. During a
  revolution, new people are drawn to politics, people who in a normal
  political process ... would never be found. They are brighter,
  sometimes not very well balanced, sometimes extremely nervous,
  often charismatic. They were too intelligent to participate in politics in
  normal times. Some were absolutely crazy (B8).
- In March 1989, I went into politics. The times then were revolutionary-
  romantic, when everything changed, when everything was different.
  It was some kind of historical watershed, a revolution, the collapse of
  communism, a time when things carried very great moral-ethical
  weight (B5).

Exculpation in these instances would seem to be purchased with
the currency of fate, but in small denominations. Revolution is
said to upset the normal order, producing a confusion which draws
unusual actors, some of whom are "absolutely crazy," into politics.
Disruption, then, can be expected to have some negative results.
Those expectations are addressed in a third line of defense that
invokes an exacting "price" to be paid for those consequences of a
revolutionary situation beyond the capacity of the revolutionaries to
prevent. They represent an aspect of fate that in this context absolves
actors of both incompetence and immorality.

- In a revolution, power uses very strong incentives, such as murder or
  the threat of murder. That is, if you don't follow orders, you'll end up in
  an urn on the shelf; if you do, you'll be king. During such
  transformations, there is often some moral price to pay. For example,
  they complain now about the absence of trust in business. The absence
  of trust means that in government and in business short-term decision

making predominates, short-term investments. This causes direct and enormous damage to the country. You have to pay this price for speed (B7).

• Any work in government subjects people to various temptations inasmuch as power inevitably gives some advantages that can be used. And many used them. Often there were cases in which great competence kept company with moral depravity. That's because such colossal social upheavals don't occur without exacting a price ... When they say now that only thieves were in that [Gaidar's] government who pilfered everything – that's untrue. They were sincere and inspired people trying for success. But, of course, they couldn't last long. When a revolutionary situation arises, dishonesty and self-enrichment proliferate, independent of what we want or don't want (C7).

CONCLUSION

This chapter has analyzed interview narratives addressing the issue of Russia's anti-communist revolution by examining their general basis in the country's political discourse and by locating them in terms of two binary structures – fate/agency and romance/anti-romance – that appear to be activated in respondents' remarks on that topic. The grid set out in Table 6.2 provides a summary of the findings. It should be emphasized, in this respect, that because my purpose has been to trace narratives back to the discursive frames in which they appear, I am not engaged here with recording individual opinions or assessments of the topic at hand, much less with computing the relative frequency of their appearance across groups in the sample. By that measure, the picture presented in the table is by no means precise. Provided with a general prompt rather than asked about revolution per se, fourteen subjects did not use the term "revolution" at all. The remaining twenty, however, did so and chose to characterize it, and to amplify those characterizations in many cases, without prompt from the interviewer. Their comments, and those of others responding to the final interview question, suggest a common discourse structured by two identifiable binaries, even while dissension reigns among them.

Table 6.2 *Positive (+) and negative (−) uses of discourse elements and binary structures concerning "revolution" across cohorts in the sample*

	Competence	Morality	Fate	Agency	Romance	Anti-romance
Gorbachev era	−	−	−*	+	−	+
First El'tsin administration	+*	+	+	+	+**	−
Second El'tsin administration	+***	+	+	+	+	−
Democratic opposition	−	−	−	+	++•	+
Putin era	−	−••	+	+	−	+

* There is one exception in this group.

** The single exception to this assessment in the first El'tsin administration would be B8, who claimed that he did not understand there to be anything "romantic about a revolution."

*** There are two mild exceptions among members of this group.

• The positive mention of "romance" by individuals in this group was invariably accompanied by expressions of disappointment, thus invoking the opposite side of the binary, "anti-romance."

•• The single exception in this group qualified his appraisal by calling the Accords "more a positive than a negative factor." He was especially critical of the competence and morality displayed by the government undertaking Russia's sociopolitical transformation.

Although the entries in Table 6.2 do not concern what individual actors might themselves "believe" or "think," and mindful of the relative heterogeneity of membership within each cohort, the results reported, here, nonetheless indicate certain regularities in the sample with respect to how various groups draw on a common discourse to take differing positions on the field of political communication. Notable, in this respect, would be the near coincidence of assessments appearing in rows one and five. With a single exception on the fate/agency binary, those in the Gorbachev-era cohort characterize Russia's recent revolution in purely negative terms. They tend to portray it as the product of incompetent agency rather than as the result of objective factors. They impute immoral motives to those regarded as responsible for it and cite as evidence the revolution's calamitous consequences. Overall, those in the Putin-era cohort concur but insist that fate played a major role in Russia's statehood, arguing in most instances that the breakup of the USSR was unavoidable, perhaps suggesting the differing positions occupied by the Gorbachev group who "lost" their country, the USSR, as opposed to the Putin-era cohort who have come to power in, and thus "gained" a country, Russia. Both groups, however, refer to the economic reforms that followed as owing little, if anything, to objective factors and were undertaken rashly and without due regard to their actual results. These findings would reinforce those reported in the preceding chapter, indicating that, across generations, professional politicians in Russia seem to share common orientations toward the political, orientations that set them sharply apart from those displayed by their nemesis, professionals in politics.

Professionals in politics are represented in rows two, three and four. Within the first two, near-unanimity prevails; the valence of all discursive elements is positive. This pattern distinguishes the narratives of these sub-sets of professionals in politics from those of professional politicians in rows one and five. But at least equally it sets them apart from the democratic opposition (displayed in row four) for whom all discursive vectors point toward the negative.

Professionals in politics comprise the ranks of this group, too, but they have not enjoyed the same position on the political field – namely, executive power – as have their counterparts in rows two and three. Thus, unsurprisingly, their narratives represent the mirror image of their liberal-democratic competitors who have held power and bear some responsibility for its use. They draw on a discourse of principled morality in order to establish a critical distance between themselves and the revolution's outcome, just as their liberal opponents – who otherwise speak this same language, as noted in the previous two chapters – tend to swerve away from it when addressing this particular topic, emphasizing fate over agency and necessity over moral principles. But it is also interesting to note in this respect how the narratives of the democratic opposition are based on the same discursive foundations as are those represented in rows one and five. Here, differences of substance appear to lie in the fact that those in the democratic opposition do not structure their remarks on revolution along the lines of "fate." Whereas those in the Putin-era cohort do so with respect to the disintegration of the USSR – thus confirming the inevitability, if not the legitimacy, of the state that they have come to govern – those in the democratic opposition tend to deny this and attribute that consequence only to incompetent and immoral agency. In this respect, their narratives resemble those in the Gorbachev group.

The narratives of the groups represented in rows one, four and five coincide on the socioeconomic aspects of Russia's transformation, albeit the invective displayed by those issuing from the Gorbachev-era cohort and the democratic opposition is not matched by those coming from the Putin-era group. The other difference distinguishing the narratives of the democratic opposition from both the Gorbachev-era and Putin-era cohorts concerns the romance/anti-romance binary. Whereas the last two groups reported no romantic attachment to the revolution, members of the democratic opposition who – unlike those in those very groups – consider themselves to have been direct participants in it, sometimes confess an involvement in this romance that led, ultimately, to the regret and disappointment associated with the other side of that binary.

The three epigrams placed at the head of this chapter represent in concentrated fashion the near-totality of positions taken by members of the sample on the question of Russia's recent revolution. In short, the messages are: it was great; it was a great disappointment; it was a great disaster. To be sure, those positions are inflected and amplified by the respondents in numerous ways: "it was great in spite of unanticipated shortcomings" and so forth. Some actually combine elements of one position with those of others. Yet those seem to be the principal positions all the same. Why? The argument here has been that within the structure of Russian political discourse, those are the positions available for taking on the field of communication. Because of the effective absence of a discourse of approval and a very stunted discourse of community, political actors almost exclusively rely on "competence" and "morality" in order to compose meaningful, intelligible utterances about the world of politics and their places in it. All, as it were, speak the same language in order to distinguish themselves and their cognitive networks not from anything so much as from one another.

These considerations supply some clues to the second puzzle under consideration here: Why has effectively no attention been paid to the public commemoration of Russia's recent revolution? One possible answer has been supplied by informant *C7* who has been quoted in Chapter 3 regarding the desirability of creating a national holiday to commemorate the defeat of the August 1991 putsch. He explained the absence of such a holiday as a consequence of the economic reform that followed which "destroyed the basic worlds of people, affecting their root, living interest." As plausible as it might be that mass material misery represents an unlikely support for political celebration, it would appear that this explanation is incomplete. A far greater degree of misery followed in the wake of the 1917 Revolution and massive commemorations nonetheless ensued.

Another possible answer would be provided by Richard Sakwa (2006) who has argued that post-communist revolutions have been both made and understood by political forces that had outgrown the notion of revolution as a dramatic rupture in time opening onto a utopian future. He claims that these more sober, anti-communist revolutions have been propelled by a different vision conveyed in the writings of those such as Havel (1985) and Michnik (1985) who intentionally blunted the revolutionary impulse in favor of a self-limiting program focused on the power of morality to transform social and political life, thus "transcending" revolution itself. To the extent that this is true, then, these revolutions would leave little ideational and emotional residue that could subsequently be employed in the service of commemoration and the marking of a new epoch. But however accurate this scenario might be for the countries of Eastern Europe, it does not seem to fit the Russian case particularly well. As noted above, political actors there still talk about revolution, still recall its romantic aspects and speak in the present about the revolutionary period as marked by a liminality including extraordinary circumstances, events and people. Moreover, anyone who experienced those three days of resistance in August 1991 likely came away with the feeling that something epochal had, indeed, occurred (Bonnell, Cooper and Freidin, 1994).

A third possible answer, specifically directed to the commem- orative neglect of the August 1991 events in Russia comes from Kathleen Smith (2002). She makes a persuasive case for a failure to inaugurate a tradition of remembrance by noting that the polarization of political forces that occurred in reaction to the onset of the eco- nomic reform launched by the government in 1992 destroyed any would-be consensus on what should be celebrated and who should be doing the celebrating. Leaders of the resistance to the August putsch found themselves on opposite sides of the barricades in 1993 – some using artillery against their erstwhile comrades-in-arms who were ensconced in the same White House that they had defended two years earlier, now under siege and then stormed by their previous political allies. The result of the analysis in this chapter, however, would amplify, if not alter, that explanation.

The dissension reviewed, above, lies not between the democrats and their communist and nationalist opponents but within the ranks of the democrats themselves. This dissension is coextensive with position-taking, and the black-and-white positions that they tend to take leave little if any room for empathetically seeing the other's point of view, let alone for reaching consensus. What is to be commemorated, a great event, a great disappointment or something even worse? This impasse results from the fact that the subjects' narratives about the revolution are framed by only two dimensions of political discourse – competence and morality – that are associated with putative *personal* qualities, themselves reflecting the *personalized* nature of political relations, use of state office and so on, as set out in the model of Civil Society *II*. In the absence of the discursive dimensions that can construct a public – community and approval – speakers are trapped in a communicative process in which each displays his/her merits and denigrates those of the other; as it were, a collective narcissism. The dialogic basis represented by the mediation of a third party, an imagined public weighing and assessing their utterances, goes missing. Thus, they are left to demonstrate their worth primarily in a negative way by assaulting the personal qualities of opponents, assaults that bring the recursive satisfaction of implicitly asserting one's own competence and morality.

7   Conclusion

Chto delat'? Kto vinovat?
[What to do? Who is to blame?]

In playfully serious tone, Russians are apt to tell their foreign
interlocutors that the questions referenced at the head of this chapter
are seminal, inescapable and eternal in their country. In so many
words, these questions seem to constitute their root terms of political
discussion, the discursive horizon of politics itself. The jesting
attitude with which these questions are often put should not disguise
the gravity that they contain, just as their exaggerated finality need
not suggest that exaggerations are not one route to the truth. Taking
those questions, then, as a point of departure, what light has this
study thrown on them? Why might they form the pivot of political
discourse in Russia?

At the outset of this book, I put forward an ideal type of
political discourse grounded on the syntax of natural language. The
argument there, and thereafter, has been that making sense is predicated on following rules, whether grammatical ones for language use
or discursive ones for political communication. In the latter instance,
however, the question of rules cannot be addressed in a purely formal
or abstract way for the simple reason that at issue is not communication in general but communication *about* something: namely, politics. Therefore, I have put forward a conception of political discourse
that models it in a substantive way. To talk about politics means to
engage with discourses of competence, morality, community and
approval. These elements in the model, moreover, are leavened by
an apprehension of politics as a "feel for the game" whose own rules
include the indefinable, the uncertain and the undecidable. The
model's elements, therefore, do not represent separate categories

exclusive of one another but discursive practices that are intertwined in the act of political speech.

The abstractness attending the model of political discourse gives it a certain breadth. In principle, it could be used to analyze political communication anywhere. However, when applied in concrete instances, the abstraction "political discourse" must be made specific in order to be at all useful in addressing its object, actual political talk. To that end, Chapter 2 developed another ideal-type model – one concerning distinct forms of social relations dubbed Civil Society *I* and *II* – in order to situate the Russian case on a field of concepts pertinent to the particular character of that social order. The implications of that exercise for narrowing the analytic focus on Russian political discourse are principally two. First, Civil Society *II* – the Russian variant – witnesses a preponderance of cultural and social capital over the economic form of same. Because those forms of capital are embodied rather than disembodied (as is characteristic of economic capital), the social relations structured by them reflect a highly personalized quality. Correspondingly, the impersonalized, abstract categories of formal equality of citizens and a rule of law governing political relations are weakly reflected in social consciousness. In their stead, strong and diffuse ties prevail among actors, making the landscape of politics an arena in which formal institutions matter little while the personal appropriation of formal offices are reticulated by sub rosa groupings called "clans" and "teams" that pursue their purposes in the effective absence of public mediation.

Second, the highly personalized character of social and political relations activates those parameters in the discursive model that refer to the personal aspects of political communication: competence and morality. Accordingly, those dimensions of political discourse oriented to the construction or thematization of a public in political speech – community and approval (law) – fall into neglect. There seems to be little in the relations of Civil Society *II* that would sustain collective, self-referential background practices that would draw on those last two discourses in order to communicate politically. To be sure, they have not been altogether absent from the narratives of those interviewed for this study, but their existence on the margins of speech renders them as weak signifiers whose only hour on stage casts them in supporting roles for one or both of the principal elements of political discourse in Russia: competence and morality. Thus, rather then serving as an institution through which the community's approval – or rejection, or disputation – is registered, law signifies formalized, general instructions issuing from the offices of those with the power to make "law." Likewise, and in correspondence with what that pattern implies for the status of citizens, community enjoys no robust representation in political speech. Rather, interview subjects characterize it generally in two ways that strip it of any agency. Either the community is depicted as the enduring but inert receiver of their benefactions, or as a degraded, uncomprehending mass who must be ruled in spite of their own desires or protests. As one respondent put it, the Russian people are portrayed by the political class as either vegetables or saints. Neither category has any comprehension of, much less business with, politics. This orientation toward the citizenry displayed by the political class is reciprocated. Countless opinion surveys regularly record the low levels of trust evinced by the citizenry toward the country's political institutions. Informal conversations reveal that this lack of trust borders on contempt, just as focus-group research has documented the alienation of voters from "their" representatives, described as altogether unconcerned with popular values and perceptions unless these need to be manipulated for electoral purposes (White, 2005; White and McAllister, 2008).

Returning to the matter at hand – why are the questions "What to do?" and "Who is to blame?" central to Russian political discourse? – the first part of an answer emerges from the discussion thus far. If social relations are to one degree or another reflected in the consciousness of participants through the medium of their background practices, then the personalized relations characteristic of Civil Society *II* are apt to be expressed by a heavy reliance on the personally oriented dimensions of political discourse: competence and morality. From the vantage of a restricted practice of political communication in which only those dimensions are fully active, they become, as it were, hyperactive, dominating and thus narrowing the communicative field. In order to enter discourse, both questions necessarily summon certain background understandings in the political community that enable issues in one instance or another to become objects of general consideration, topics of discussion. For example, "What to do?" is at bottom a question about competence. Although the shadow of morality also hangs over it – inasmuch as it implies that the thing to do would be the right one – the issue of competence is more ramified in this regard, thus giving speakers more to talk about. In the course of addressing it, four presuppositions become activated: (1) there is a problem and something, indeed, needs to be done about it; (2) there actually is something that can be done about the problem; (3) someone can or does know what that something is; and (4) the questioner may himself be that someone, implying as much by the fact that he has raised the question "What to do?" just as Lenin ([1902] 1969) did by giving this title to his famous work on building a party in order to make a revolution. With these background understandings in place, parties to communication have already constructed a format for unfolding a discourse of competence. They enact that discourse by supplying criteria pertinent to their respective stocks of cultural capital and their positions on the political field. Consequently some insist that it is professionals who know what to do, while others contend that those professionals in charge of things have got it wrong (thus implying that they could get it right), while yet others maintain that it is professional politicians who have the answer to the problem. Replies may be extended by, say, asserting the importance of assimilating new institutions and practices ("democracy" or "the market") or duly appreciating the importance of domestic forms of intercourse ("our traditions and culture" or "democracy in Russia is *sobornost'*"). But the underpinning is still the same: whether a claim by some that they possess the competence to introduce new institutions, or a counterclaim by others insisting that they are able to recognize established patterns and thereby direct matters more effectively by virtue of that knowledge.

"Who is to blame?" is about morality. Of course, blame-laying could also include charges of incompetence, but such a query does not give speakers much to talk about in that respect. Rather, like its partner, this particular question indexes four background understandings about morality that make it intelligible to the parties in communication, thereby constructing their discursive practices. "Who is to blame?" connotes: (1) a situation in which the normative order has been violated; (2) that someone is responsible for this violation; (3) that this someone has not acted morally; and (4) that those accusing this someone have opened the way to a restoration of the normative order and are therefore acting morally themselves. Grounding their narratives on these considerations, respondents in this study rely on moral discourse to accuse others and to absolve themselves. They accomplish this in a number of ways, but their statements on morality can be located on a single continuum bounded at either end by conflicting versions of morality, each associated with the type of cultural capital in the possession of the speaker, conditioned by his position on the political field. At one end of the continuum lies a version of morality that features impersonal, abstract principles said to guide one's own action and to recognize its absence in the actions of others. This form of moral discourse tends to prevail among those who entered politics from professional, usually academic, careers. It is especially pronounced among members of that same group who have experienced the greatest remove from power and who, in a number of instances, express pride in their marginalization or, indeed, in having eschewed power itself. Moral discourse of this sort involves the demand for more morality in government and politics, a demand that is endless in the face of the absence of a legal culture capable of integrating individuals into a normative order, complete with effective sanctions, that regulates their conduct. To that extent, this form of moral discourse is based on misrecognition. On one hand, it presupposes that the other *should* conform to the moral code expressed by the subject. Despite continuous experience to the contrary, the subject nonetheless insists upon repeating that injunction and upon castigating the other when, again, the injunction is not honored. On the other hand, it places the subject himself somehow outside or above the very "immoral" world indexed by the rebuke of immorality. "Who is to blame?" is not a reflexive question answerable by "me." Simply asking it can be a form of self-absolution.

At the other pole of moral discourse in Russian politics lies loyalty. This conception is at home amid the personalized relations characteristic of Civil Society *II* in which trust is a scarce commodity carefully husbanded by those who have established strong ties with each other in "clans" or "teams." Loyalty thus opens onto practical matters, appearing as the indispensable lubricant for collective action. This form of moral discourse, however, is not self-contained. It remains mindful of its polar opposite by negating it discursively with the language of practice. Its alibis are the exigencies of the political world and the necessity of getting "results," the practical criterion proffered to sustain any discussion of morality in politics.

The split in moral discourse characteristic of the political class parallels a comparable division in their discourse of competence. "Professionalism" is the principal signifier of that desideratum, but the term admits to two diametrically opposed meanings, each a reflection of the form of capital that its users prize most. For one group, professionalism connotes expert knowledge that they claim to bring to government and politics. They are the ones who know what is to be done, an assertion reflecting the cultural capital that is in the possession of the speaker. That assertion rests not only on professional credentials per se, but also on the connotations of disinterestedness associated with them. This form of capital thus exchanges for political power as a valued commodity insured by a users' warranty – knowledge that can be relied upon because its purveyor has no interest beyond applying that knowledge for the benefit of others.

For the other group, "professionalism" spells *political* know-how, the ability to achieve results in that practical world referenced in their habitus. This claim to political power issues from another form of capital; namely, social capital that connects persons in power networks. As outlined in Chapter 5, the construction of this group's identity as professional politicians represents the mirror image of that of their competitors – professionals in politics – whose primary form of capital is cultural rather than social. From this vantage, two distinct cultures of power are evident. Each is expressed by means of discursive strategies, rooted in group habitus, that concern the accumulation and exchange of its particular form of capital. Thus, a discourse of morality emphasizing impersonal norms combines with a discourse of competence based on disinterested knowledge to construct a political identity anchored in cultural capital, just as discourses of competence as know-how and morality as situational undergird a political identity based on social capital. As noted in the foregoing, however, subjects are not locked into a single version of political discourse, whether they are professionals in politics or professional politicians. The former sometimes ruminate on their own lack of know-how and cite it as the reason for missing important opportunities while they were in government. The later, likewise, draw on historical and cultural categories to justify or explain their own actions in the world, thus relying on the language of their opposite numbers, professionals.

Chapters 3 through 5 have each been organized around the constituent elements of contemporary Russian political discourse by pulling from the interview texts narratives that concern the themes of community, morality (and law) and competence. Chapter 6, however, represents a departure from this analytic pattern by throwing all of the elements into play simultaneously in order to investigate how those cultures of power identified in the interview results combine them into discrete discursive strategies for addressing, characterizing and evaluating issues related to a single topic. The focus, there, falls on the most significant event in Russian politics to have occurred within the time frame of this study – revolution – and on the various positions taken on it by members of the sample. Because of the overall weight of competence and morality in Russian political discourse generally, the particular narrative programs associated with the positions taken on the revolution tend, again, to divide the actors into mutually antagonistic camps. Here, the relative absence of discourses of community and approval have telling effect. They are not on hand to mediate among the positions taken by the actors by drawing in an imagined third party, the public, that might serve as a sounding board against which statements can be assessed. Therefore, subjects address one another directly, so to speak, from the positions that they have taken, using the discursive means available to them: once again, competence and morality. On that basis, narratives become truncated into various versions of praise, blame and excuses. Someone is held to be competent or not, moral or immoral. Assessments and appraisals along those lines attempt to account for what happened and why. The distances separating the positions asserted and defended on that basis are unbridgeable to the point that subjects do not concur on when the revolution began and ended, much less on what actually happened – reform or theft, independence or treason – or what it means for Russia's future. The Babel of the political class is reflected in the country's symbolic order as a blank spot: no public commemoration of the most important political event to have occurred in the lifetimes of its citizens.

Position-taking on the matter of revolution generally coincides with membership in one of the five cohorts identified in the sample. For example, in the same way that Gorbachev- and Putin-era groups embrace a common notion of competence and morality characteristic of professional politicians, they likewise tend to view the revolution as the doing of incompetent and immoral leaders who sold out the country (the USSR) and impoverished its citizens. These are broadsides fired by holders of social capital at their counterparts in the El'tsin administrations who are in possession of the cultural variety. Those counterparts return the fire, arguing that it was they who were able to recognize necessity and to take actions that rescued the country (Russia) and its citizens from the threat of famine and nuclear war. The third position on the revolution is occupied by members of the democratic opposition, Yabloko. Although this contingent has been regarded by effectively all political observers as positioned in closest ideological proximity to the El'tsin-era cohorts – a view reinforced by numerous (albeit almost uniformly futile) efforts on both sides to cooperate if not to unify – the position that they take on the revolution in fact places them furthest from the El'tsin-era groups. Not only do they share with the Gorbachev- and Putin-era respondents the same negative assessments of competence and morality, but they introduce elements of sorrow and rage in their remarks specific to themselves as those who had collaborated in a cause that they came to regard as betrayed. Whereas Gorbachev- and Putin-era subjects, inasmuch as they were not involved with leading this revolution themselves, describe and assess events from a certain distance, the remarks made by those in the democratic opposition index the fact that they had been in the thick of things. Most of them had been engaged with the democratic movement during the political struggles that had begun under *perestroika*. A number of them had risked their lives in the defense of Russian democracy during the coup attempt of August 1991. They thus recall their own romantic attachments to the revolution whose dashed expectations became the basis for reconstructing their identities as a democratic opposition.

This review of position-taking among subjects on the matter of revolution would indicate that ideological affinity is an indeterminate thing. From the perspective of individuals in possession of beliefs and values, one would expect to find the greatest agreement on the significance and implications of Russia's recent revolution registered by the El'tsin-era cohorts and the democratic opposition. In fact, the opposite is the case. Of course, differences in access to power – and along with it, responsibility for that which has occurred – would represent an important situational factor that might account for this division. However, recalling how members of the democratic opposition have spoken with pride about both declining and resigning government office, it cannot explain the very thing said to be doing the explaining: the difference in access itself. The approach adopted in this book would regard that difference as the manifestation of deeper ones drawn by the discursive interactions of actors on the field of politics. Parties to those interactions are not at liberty, at least insofar as they would continue to participate in those same interactions by saying things intelligible to one another, to say what they please. Rather, their narratives are confined to the discourses available for their use. In the same way, the positions that they carve out for themselves on the field of politics at bottom represent selections – sometimes creatively adapted ones – from among the possible set of positions generated by the discursive interactions of all the parties. As the issue of access to power or its refusal reminds, in politics it would seem that words do not follow the facts so much as facts follow the words.

The methodology employed in this book differs fundamentally from that encountered in conventional works on comparative politics and, in particular, in those devoted to the study of politics in Russia. It has attempted to reconstruct the subjectivity of a political class rather than to analyze "objective" phenomena such as formal institutions, causal factors or behavior per se that have been topics more familiar to this field and area of study. Accordingly, the focus here has fallen on language as an avenue to culture and consciousness, to the meanings that politics holds for those acting in that world. What advantages might be claimed for this alternative approach? Although, in the end, others are in better position to make that assessment, I would argue that a discursive construction of the political has the capacity to shed light on critical, yet neglected or imperfectly understood, aspects of politics. Because I am by no means the first to make this claim and because this book itself has already set out my reasons for making it, there is no point in revisiting the matter at this stage. Instead, I wish to conclude with two illustrations that came out of the present study, which show how this alternative construction of the political might pay dividends. One concerns Russian politics directly, the other, the broader field of comparative studies. Both involve core issues for comparative politics: democracy and authoritarianism. Each, in turn, speaks to a palpable and, as I judge it, growing discontent in the comparative field with the positivist underpinnings of conventional approaches and their attendant constrictions on how those core issues can be framed.

The first implication involves accounting for the persistence of authoritarian rule in Russia. That is, despite massive changes in regime over the past century, from tsarism to communism to republicanism, authoritarianism has persistently characterized the prevailing political order. Why? To be sure, plenty of reasons can be, and have been, adduced to explain this – history, geography, culture, the weakness of civil society, and others – and it is not my purpose to refute any of them here. Rather, I want to offer a reason for this phenomenon that comes into view from the perspective of discourse analysis advanced in this study. That reason concerns absences: namely, those of community and approval – the public dimensions of political language – that scarcely figure in the language of the country's political elite. Beyond merely recording this absence, which itself would be little more than listing another way in which Russia does not measure up on the democratic yardstick, the framing of Russian politics as a discursive community would in this instance underscore the impossibility of realizing one of democracy's prerequisites: *viz.*, the communicative space required for an opposition to exist. In the same way that democracy is unthinkable without an opposition, so that opposition must be part of, or "loyal" to, some entity greater than either itself or that which it opposes. Loyal to what? If not to the sovereign, himself, then to the construct of a "sovereign people." Without that construct, opposition can only appear as the enemy of power. It serves no purpose or master higher than itself. Power is thus not discursively required to accept it, to recognize it, as anything but disloyal to that very power. Consequently, the opposition is there to be stopped, and power acts accordingly. Authoritarian politics is the direct result.

The second implication concerns another absence, this one in what otherwise is a promising literature that has been emerging in comparative politics on the issue of democratization. That absence is the insufficient attention paid by students of this subject to elite political discourse. Disturbed by the dominance in the field of a formulaic and constricting definition of what counts for democracy – represented above all by the theorizing of Joseph Schumpeter (1962) and Adam Przeworski (1991) – a number of scholars influenced by ethnology and cultural studies have adopted an approach to this question that expands the analytic horizon by focusing on democratic practices occurring in just those places where the conventional approach is unlikely to look for them. Examples would include the sociability attending qat chews in Yemen, where most men seem to gather daily for the stimulation provided both by the herb itself and by hours-long deliberations on matters of common interest, thus enacting their version of the French salons in which that country's republican movement was birthed (Wedeen, 2008). Comparable political practices occurring within the context of both formal and informal bodies at some remove from state power have been documented in Latin American cultural politics during the years of dictatorship (Alvarez, Dagnino and Escaban, 1998), and in African processes of grass-roots deliberation and consultation under authoritarian governments (Chabal and Daloz, 2006). In China, homeowners' associations (Read, 2008) and internet-based environmental activists (Gilboy and Read, 2008) have displayed a distinctly political potential, while in Russia longstanding patterns of friendship may be capable of providing newfound models for relations in the public sphere (Kharkhordin, 2009b).

Works such as these concerning politics in everyday life have enriched the concept of democracy by re-framing it as a condition of society rather than merely as a system of government. In so doing, these studies alert us to important, perhaps critical, factors shaping the political world, factors that would be obscure if not invisible from the positivist perspective on democratization that has hitherto dominated the field. However, this welcome expansion of vista seems to be tacitly predicated on a supposition that these proto-politics have a trajectory – that they are leading somewhere: *viz.*, to democracy. This assumption appears to account for the attention paid to these practices, re-framing them as topics for *political* investigation. In this respect, the present volume may have a contribution to make by clarifying a condition impinging on that assumption itself. That is, if these everyday (political) practices are to contribute to a transformation of the larger political order in the direction of democracy, then they must be absorbed into the language of politics as phenomena occurring not simply among some sector of the population but practices characteristic of "the people," that imagined entity at the center of political discourse in a democratic state. The Russian case would throw up a caution in that regard. Despite the fact that an everyday politics of deliberation is alive and well in that country – as too many kitchen conversations or chats about politics struck up with strangers would prevent me from denying – no one among Western observers these days seems to display the sort of optimism characteristic of the 1990s about the prospects for democratization there. As I have shown in the foregoing, the Russian case reveals a critical consideration for the progress of democratic transformation: a space within elite political discourse for the immaterial power of the people.

Appendix: Sketches of respondents' backgrounds

BAKATIN, Vadim Viktorovich. Born 1937 in Kiselevsk, Kemerovo Oblast'. Graduated from the Novosibirsk Engineering-Construction Institute in 1960 and the Academy of Social Sciences of the Central Committee of the CPSU in 1985. Served as: secretary of the Kemerovo Oblast' Committee of the CPSU (1977–1983) and as its first secretary (1987–1988); thereafter as Minister of Internal Affairs USSR until 1990; as Chairperson of the KGB from August 1991 until its abolition in October; and as Chairperson of the Inter-Republican Security Service (successor to KGB) from October till December 1991.

BAKHMIN, Vyacheslav Ivanovich. Born 1947 in Tver'. Studied at the Moscow Physics-Technical Institute (1966–1970) and graduated from the Correspondence Division of the Moscow Economics-Statistics Institute (1974). Since 1968, a participant in the human rights movement. Headed the Department of Global Problems and Humanitarian Cooperation, Ministry of Foreign Affairs, Russian Soviet Federated Socialist Republic (RSFSR) from 1991 to 1992, and the Department of International Humanitarian and Cultural Cooperation of the Ministry of Foreign Affairs of the Russian Federation (1992–1995).

BOLDYREV, Yurii Yur'evich. Born 1960 in Leningrad. Graduated from the Leningrad Electro-Technical Institute (1983) and Leningrad Financial-Economics Institute (1989). Elected people's deputy of the USSR (1989–1991). Headed Control Administration of the President of the Russian Federation (1992–1993). Elected: deputy to the Council of the Federation (1993–1995) as a leader of the Yabloko electoral organization (1993–1995); Deputy Chair of the Accounting Chamber of the Federal Assembly of the Russian Federation (1995–2001).

BURBULIS, Gennadii Eduardovich. Born 1945 in Sverdlovsk Oblast'. Graduated from the Philosophy Faculty of Sverdlovsk State

University (1974) and received a candidate's degree from the Urals Polytechnic Institute (1981). Elected people's deputy of the USSR (1989–1991). Directed Boris El'tsin's presidential campaign and named First Deputy Prime Minister of the RSFSR (1991–1992), State Secretary of the RSFSR (1991–1992) and deputy chair of the President's Consulting Council (1992). Elected deputy to State Duma (1993–1999) and named to the Council of the Federation (2001–).

DANILOV-DANIL'YAN, Viktor Ivanovich. Born 1938 in Moscow. Graduated from the Mechanical-Mathematics Faculty of Moscow State University (1960), taking candidate's (1966) and doctoral degrees (1973) there. Acting Deputy Minster of the Environment and Use of Natural Resources of USSR (1991), and of the RSFSR (1991–1996). Elected to State Duma (1993–1995) and chaired State Committee of the Russian Federation for Environmental Preservation (1996–2000).

GAIDAR, Egor Timurovich. Born 1956 in Moscow. Graduated in economics from Moscow State University (1978), taking a candidate's degree there in 1980. Named Deputy Prime Minister and Minister of Economics and Finance (1991–1992, 1993) and Acting Prime Minister (1992) of the RSFSR. Led the party Russia's Choice (1993–1994) and co-led Union of Right Forces (1999–2004). Elected deputy to State Duma (1993–1995, 1999–2003). Identified as architect of post-communist economic reform in Russia.

GOLOV, Anatolii Grigor'evich. Born 1946 in Moscow Oblast'. Graduated from the Mathematics-Mechanical Faculty of Leningrad State University (1968). Elected to Leningrad Soviet (1990) and to State Duma (1993–2003); one of the leaders of the Social Democratic Party of Russia (1990–1996) and of the Leningrad (St. Petersburg) division of Democratic Russia (1991–1993).

GRIGOR'EV, Oleg Vadimovich. Born 1960 in Moscow. Graduated in economic cybernetics from Moscow State University (1982). Consultant to factions in the Supreme Soviet, RSFSR (1989–1993); deputy leader of the staff of the State Duma (1994–1997); division head, Administration of the President (1997–1998).

GRIGOR'EV, Leonid Markovich. Born 1947 in Moscow. Graduated from the Economics Faculty of Moscow State University (1968), receiving a candidate's degree there in 1973 and later a teaching position (1991). Deputy Minister of the Economy (1991–1992); Deputy Director of International Bank for Reconstruction and Development, Moscow branch (1992–1993) and chief advisor there (1993–1997).

IVANOV, Evgenii Viktorovich. Born 1964. Graduated in history from Kuban State University (1987) and in advertising from the Russian University of the Friendship of the Peoples. Department head, Ministry of Nationalities (1994–1995); deputy to head of Russian occupation government in Chechnya (1995–1996); assistant head of the Administration of the President (1996–1997); vice-governor Krasnoyarsk Krai (2002–2003). Elected to State Duma on list of Liberal Democratic Party of Russia (2003–).

IGRUNOV, Vyacheslav Vladimirovich. Born 1948 in Zhitomir Oblast'. Repressed, and did not complete degree at Odessa Institute of the National Economy. Underground political work (1965–1970), dissident activity (1970–1974), arrested (1975) and sent to psychiatric hospital and labor camp, freed in 1977. Moved to Moscow in 1987, taking up publicist and organizational work with democratic movement. Founding member of Yabloko, its deputy leader (1996–2000), thrice elected on its list to State Duma (1993–2003).

ISAEV, Andrei Konstantinovich. Born 1964 in Moscow. Graduated in history from Moscow State Pedagogical Institute (1989), where he participated in an underground political group, leading to the anarchist group, *Obshchina*, that he led de facto. Participated in anarchist and, later, labor organizations. Elected to State Duma (1999–) and became one of the leaders of the United Russia faction (2001–).

KHOVANSKAYA, Galina Petrovna. Born 1943 in Moscow. Graduated from the Moscow Physical Engineering Institute (1966) and the Institute of State and Law (1996). Began organizational work in the democratic movement in 1989; elected to district soviet (1990–1993), City Council of Moscow (1993–2003) and to State Duma (2003).

KOLESNIKOV, Sergei Vladimirovich. Born 1952. Graduated in history from Moscow State University (1974), taking a candidate's degree there in 1979. Following a journalistic career, he joined the Russian government as advisor to prime ministers E. Gaidar and V. Chernomyrdin (1991–1996) and later to prime minister M. Fradkov (2004).

KOVALEV, Andrei Anatol'evich. Candidate of historical studies. Career foreign service officer. Speech writer and foreign policy consultant to General Secretary of CPSU, M. S. Gorbachev, 1986–1991. Acting director of department, Russian Ministry of Foreign Affairs, 1991–1992.

KUVALDIN, Viktor Borisovich. Born 1943 in Moscow. Graduated in law from Moscow State University (1965), taking candidate's (1969) and doctoral degrees (1984) there. Consultant to and speechwriter for CPSU leader M. S. Gorbachev (1989–1991) and director of his presidential campaign (1996).

LAVROVSKII, Igor' Kaml'evich. Academy of Sciences, USSR, sector on energy policy for Soviet government, 1986–1987. Journalist for *Socialist Industry*, 1987–1988. Graduate education and oil consulting, Alberta, Canada 1988–1999. Journalist with *Nezavisimaya gazeta*, 1999–2001. Director of the Ideological Administration of the Central Executive Committee of United Russia, 2001–.

MIRONENKO, Viktor Ivanonvich. Born 1953 in Ukraine. Graduated in history from Chernigov Pedagogical Institute 1974. Served as: leader of the Ukranian Communist Union of Youth (1983–1986) and All-Union Communist Union of Youth (1986–1990); candidate member of the Central Committee of the CPSU (1986–1988), full member (1988–1990); first deputy head of CPSU department (1990–1991).

MITROKHIN, Sergei Sergeevich. Born 1963 in Moscow. Graduated in philology from Moscow State Pedagogical Institute in 1985. Active in informal politics (1987–1989). Elected to State Duma on the Yabloko list (1993–2003) and Moscow City Council (2005–). Deputy leader of Yabloko (2000–).

MOROZOV, Oleg Viktorovich. Born 1953 in Kazan. Graduated in history from Kazan State University (1971) where he later took a candidate's degree. Regional, then national staff work in the CPSU (1987–1991). Deputy to State Duma (1994–). A leader of the political factions and parties: Regions of Russia (1995–1999); Fatherland-All Russia (1999–2001); United Russia (2002–).

MURASHEV, Arkadii Nikolaevich. Born 1957 in Poland. Graduated in engineering from Bauman Technical University in Moscow (1980). Elected people's deputy of the USSR (1989–1991). Served as police chief of Moscow (1991) and as a principal organizer of the Inter-Regional Deputies Group (1989–1991), Democratic Russia (1991–1992), Russia's Choice (1993) and the Union of Right Forces (2000–2001). Deputy of the State Duma (1993–1995).

NAISHUL', Vitalii Arkad'evich. Born 1949 in Moscow. Graduated from the Mechanical-Mathematics Faculty of Moscow State University (1971), and then held research positions in Gosplan USSR and Central Economics-Mathematics Institute. Political career as publicist and economics advisor to members of El'tsin's government and presidential candidate A. Lebed (1996).

NECHAEV, Andrei Alekseevich. Born 1953 in Moscow. Graduated in economics from Moscow State University (1975), taking a candidate's degree there in 1978. Named First Deputy Minister of Economics and Finance of RSFSR (1991), Minister of Economics (1992). Active in banking industry and Russia's Business Round Table since 1994.

PIKHOYA, Ludmila Grigor'evna. Born 1946 in Sverdlovsk. Graduated in history from Urals State University (1968) where she took a candidate's degree in 1984. Joined B. El'tsin's election campaign in 1990 and served as his principal speechwriter until 1998.

PLIGIN, Vladimir Nikolaevich. Born 1960 in Vologda. Graduated in law from Leningrad State University. After pursuing a legal career, elected to State Duma on the United Russia list (2003–) where he chairs the Committee on Constitutional Law and State Construction.

SATAROV, Georgii Aleksandrovich. Born 1947 in Moscow. Graduated in mathematics from Moscow State Pedagogical Institute (1972) where he took a candidate's degree in 1985. Co-founded the Center of Applied Political Research and directed it (1990–1993, 1997–). Named to Presidential Council (1993), then assistant to the president (1994) and served in a variety of policymaking and political roles in the Administration of the President till 1997.

SHAKHRAI, Sergei Mikhailovich. Born 1956 in Simferopol. Graduated in law from Rostov University and received a candidate's degree from Moscow State University in 1982. Elected people's deputy of the RSFSR (1990–1992), chairing Committee on Legislation. Named to State Council of the RSFSR (1991–1993) and served as principal author of its constitutional projects and treaty creating CIS. Appointed Deputy Prime Minister of the RSFSR (1991–1995), member of Security Council (1992–1993) and Minister of Nationalities (1993–1994). Leader of Party of Russian Unity and Accord (1993–1995), deputy of State Duma (1993–1995), deputy head of the Accounting Chamber (2000–).

SHEINIS, Viktor Leonidovich. Born 1931 in Kiev. Graduated in law from Leningrad State University (1953) and took a candidate's degree in economics there in 1966. Doctoral degree from the Institute of the World Economy and International Relations (1982). Active in informal politics (1988–1990). Elected people's deputy of the RSFSR (1990–1993) and deputy of the State Duma on the Yabloko list (1993–2003).

SMIRNYAGIN, Leonid Viktorovich. Born 1935. Graduated in geography from Moscow State University (1958) where he later took a doctorate (2005). Served on the Presidential Council (1993–1997).

TSIPKO, Aleksandr Sergeevich. Born 1941 in Odessa. Graduated in philosophy from Moscow State University (1968). Consultant to Central Committee of the CPSU on Polish affairs (1981–1990) and assistant to CPSU Secretary A. Yakovlev (1988–1990). Thereafter, active as publicist, academic and political organizer.

URNOV, Mark Yur'evich. Born 1947 in Moscow. Graduated in economics from the Moscow Institute of International Relations (1970). After taking a candidate's degree, he pursued an academic and consulting career before joining the Administration of the President, serving as head of the Analytic Administration (1994–1996).

VASIL'EV, Sergei Aleksandrovich. Born 1957 in Leningrad. Graduated from the Leningrad Financial-Economics Institute (1979), taking a candidate's degree there in 1984. Participated in informal political organizations (1987–1989), elected to Leningrad City Council (1990–1991) and then moved to Moscow in 1991 where he was designated Head of the Working Center of Economic Reforms of the Russian Federation. Named Deputy Minister of the Economy (1994–1997), deputy head of government staff (1998) and member of the Council of the Federation (2001–).

YAVLINSKII, Grigorii Alekseevich. Born 1952 in Lviv. Graduated from the Moscow Institute of the National Economy (1976), where he later earned candidate's and doctoral degrees. The principal author of the reform program "500 Days," rejected by the USSR and temporarily accepted by the RSFSR (1990). Retired as Deputy Prime Minister of Russia (1990). Party leader of Yabloko (1993–) and deputy of State Duma (1993–2003); candidate for the Russian presidency in 1996 and 2000, placed fourth and third, respectively, in the balloting.

YASIN, Evgenii Grigor'evich. Born 1934 in Odessa. Graduated from the Odessa Construction Institute (1957) and took an economics degree at Moscow State University (1963) and candidate's (1968) and doctoral degrees (1973) there. Headed Department of Economic Reform of the USSR's Council of Ministers (1989–1991) and worked in a similar capacity for the Russian government and presidency (1992–1994). Named Minister of Economics (1994–1997) and minister without portfolio (1997–1998).

References

Afanas'ev, M. N. 2000. *Klientelizm i rossisskaya gosudarstvennost'*. 2nd edn. Moscow: Moskovskii obshchestvennyi nauchnyi fond.

Afanas'ev, Yu. N. (ed.) 1988. *Inogo ne dano*. Moscow: Progress.

Aksartova, Sada. 2005. "Civil Society from Abroad: U.S. Donors in the Former Soviet Union." Doctoral dissertation, Princeton University.

Almond, Gabriel, and Sidney Verba. 1963. *The Civic Culture*. Princeton: Princeton University Press.

Alvarez, Sonia, Evelino Dagnino, and Arturo Escobar (eds.). 1998. *Culture of Politics, Politics of Culture*. Boulder, CO: Westview.

Anderson, Benedict. 1983. *Imagined Communities: Reflections on the Origin and Spread of Nationalism*. London: Verso/NLB.

Anderson, Richard. 2001. "The Discursive Origins of Russian Democratic Politics," R. Anderson *et al.* (eds.), *Postcommunism and the Theory of Democracy*. Princeton: Princeton University Press: 96–125.

Anon. [2005]. "Sons of Russian Functionaries Go into Business." *Vedomosti* (in Johnson's Russia List, April 4, 2005).

Arendt, Hannah. (1963)1982. *On Revolution*. New York: Greenwood.

Bandelj, Nina. 2002. "Embedded Economics: Social Relations as Determinants of Foreign Direct Investment in Central and Eastern Europe," *Social Forces* 81 (no. 2): 411–444.

Barnes, Andrew. 2006. *Owning Russia: The Struggle Over Factories, Farms and Power*. Ithaca: Cornell University Press.

Barthes, Roland. 1968. *Elements of Semiology*. New York: Hill and Wang.

Barthes, Roland. 1972. *Mythologies*. New York: Hill and Wang.

Baturin, Yu. M. *et al.* 2001. *Epokha E'ltsina: ocherki: politicheskoi istorii*. Moscow: Vagrius.

Baumgartner, Frank, and Ruth Leech. 1998. *Basic Interests: The Importance of Groups in Politics and in Political Science*. Princeton: Princeton University Press.

Berman, Harold. 1961. *Justice in the USSR*. Cambridge, MA: Harvard University Press.

Berman, Sheri. 1997. "Civil Society and the Collapse of the Weimar Republic," *World Politics* 49 (no. 3): 401–429.

Bermeo, Nancy, and Philip Nord (eds.). 2000. *Civil Society before Democracy: Lessons from Nineteenth-Century Europe.* Lanham, MD: Rowman and Littlefield.

Biryukov, Nikolai, and Victor Sergeyev. 1993. "Parliamentarianism and *Sobornost'*: Two Models of Representative Institutions in Russian Political Culture," *Discourse & Society* 4 (no. 1): 57–74.

Biryukov, Nikolai, Jeffrey Gleisner, and Victor Sergeyev. 1995. "The Crisis of *Sobornost'*: Parliamentary Discourse in Present-Day Russia," *Discourse & Society* 6 (no. 2): 149–171.

Bonnell, Victoria, Ann Cooper, and Gregory Freidin (eds.). 1994. *Russia at the Barricades: Eyewitness Accounts of the August 1991 Coup.* Armonk, NY: M. E. Sharpe.

Bourdieu, Pierre. 1977. *Outline of a Theory of Practice.* Cambridge: Cambridge University Press.

Bourdieu, Pierre. 1984. *Distinction: A Social Critique of the Judgement of Taste.* Cambridge: Harvard University Press.

Bourdieu, Pierre. 1986. "The Forms of Capital," J. G. Richardson (ed.), *The Handbook of Theory and Research for the Sociology of Education.* New York: Greenwood: 241–258.

Bourdieu, Pierre. 1990. *In Other Words.* Cambridge: Polity Press.

Bourdieu, Pierre. 1993. *The Field of Cultural Production,* R. Johnson (ed.). New York: Columbia University Press.

Bourdieu, Pierre. 1998. *Practical Reason: On the Theory of Action.* Stanford: Stanford University Press.

Bourdieu, Pierre. 1999. "Rethinking the State: Genesis and Structure of the Bureaucratic Field," G. Steinmetz (ed.), *State/Culture: State Formation after the Cultural Turn.* Ithaca: Cornell University Press: 53–75.

Bourdieu, Pierre. 2005. "Habitus," J. Hiller and E. Rooksbe (eds.), *Habitus: A Sense of Place.* 2nd edn. Aldershot, UK: Ashgate: 43–49.

Bourdieu, Pierre. 2008. *Sketch for a Self-Analysis.* Chicago: University of Chicago Press.

Bourmeyster, Alexandre. 1983, "Utopie, ideologie et skaz," *Essais sur le discours soviétique,* no. 3: 1–53.

Bova, Russell. 1991. "Political Dynamics of the Post-Communist Transition: A Comparative Perspective," *World Politics* 44 (October): 117–134.

Boym, Svetlana. 2001. *The Future of Nostalgia.* New York: Basic Books.

Breslauer, George. 2001. "Personalism Versus Proceduralism: Boris Yeltsin and the Institutional Fragility of the Russian System," V. Bonnell and G. Breslauer (eds.), *Russia in the New Century: Stability or Disorder*. Boulder, CO: Westview: 35–58.

Buck, Andrew. 2007. "Elite Networks and Worldviews during the Yel'tsin Years," *Europe–Asia Studies* 59 (June): 643–661.

Burawoy, Michael. 2004. "For a Sociological Marxism: The Complementary Convergence of Antonio Gramsci and Karl Polanyi," *Politics & Society* 37 (June): 193–246.

Carothers, Thomas, and Marine Ottaway. 2000. "The Burgeoning World of Civil Society Aid," M. Ottoway and T. Carothers (eds.), *Funding Virtue: Civil Society and the Democracy Promotion*. Washington, DC: Carnegie Endowment for International Peace: 3–7.

Cassirer, Ernst. 1944. *An Essay on Man*. New York: Doubleday.

Cassirer, Ernst. 1946. *Language and Myth*. New York: Dover.

Casula, Philipp, and Jeronim Perovic (eds.). 2009. *Identities and Politics during the Putin Presidency: The Foundations of Russia's Stability*. Stuttgart: Ibidem.

Chabal, Patrick, and Jean-Pascal Dalos. 2006. *Culture Troubles: Politics and the Interpretation of Meaning*. London: Hurst & Co.

Clark, Katerina. 1995. *Petersburg: Crucible of Cultural Revolution*. Cambridge, MA: Harvard University Press.

Coleman, James. 1990. *Foundations of Social Theory*. Cambridge, MA: Belknap.

Connerton, Paul. 1989. *How Societies Remember*. Cambridge: Cambridge University Press.

Daugavet, A. B. 2003. "Opyt kognitivnogo podkhoda k izuchniyu instituta vlastnoi elity," A. Duka (ed.), *Vlast' i elity v sovremennoi Rossii*. St. Petersburg: Kovalevskii Sociological Society: 63–91.

Derluguian, Georgi. 2003. *Bourdieu's Secret Admirer in the Caucasus: A World-System Biography*. Chicago: University of Chicago Press.

Diamond, Larry. 1994. "Rethinking Civil Society: Toward Democratic Consolidation," *Journal of Democracy* 5 (no. 3): 4–17.

Djankov, Simeon. 2004. "Entrepreneurship: First Results from Russia". World Bank, http://www.worldbank.org/finance/assets/images/Entrepreneurship Russia.pdf (November).

Edelman, Murray. 1977. *Political Language*. New York: Academic Press.

Edelman, Murray. 1988. *Constructing the Political Spectacle*. Chicago: University of Chicago Press.

Ehrenberg, John. 1999. *Civil Society: The Critical History of an Idea*. New York: New York University Press.

Ekiert, Grzegorz, and Jan Kubik. 1999. *Rebellious Civil Society: Popular Protest and Democratic Consolidation in Poland 1989–1993*. Ann Arbor: University of Michigan Press.

Encarnacion, Omar. 2003. *The Myth of Civil Society: Social Capital and Democratic Consolidation in Spain and Brazil*. New York: Palgrave Macmillan.

Encarnacion, Omar. 2006. "Civil Society Reconsidered," *Comparative Politics* 38 (April): 357–376.

Epstein, Charlotte. 2008. *The Power of Words in International Relations: Birth of an Anti-Whaling Discourse*. Cambridge, MA: MIT Press.

Eyal, Gil, Ivan Szelenyi, and Eleanor Townsley. 1998. *Making Capitalism without Capitalists: The New Ruling Elites in Eastern Europe*. London: Verso.

Fazullina, Guzel. 2004. "State Officials Are Going into Business," *Rodnaya gazeta*, November 12 (in Johnson's Russia List, Nov. 15, 2004).

Flap, Henk, and Beate Volker. 2003. "Communist Societies, the Velvet Revolution and Weak Ties," G. Badescu and E. Uslaner (eds.), *Social Capital and the Transition to Democracy*. London: Routledge: 28–45.

Fleron, Frederic. 1996. "Post-Soviet Political Culture in Russia: An Assessment of Recent Empirical Investigations," *Europe–Asia Studies* 48 (March): 225–260.

Foley, Michael, and Bob Edwards. 1997a. "Escape From Politics? Social Theory and the Social Capital Debate," *American Behavioral Scientist* 40 (March/April): 550–561.

Foley, Michael, and Bob Edwards. 1997b. "Social Capital and the Political Economy of Our Discontent," *American Behavioral Scientist* 40 (March/April): 669–678.

Foley, Michael, and Bob Edwards. 1998a. "Beyond Tocqueville: Civil Society and Social Capital in Comparative Perspective," *American Behavioral Scientist* 42 (September): 5–20.

Foley, Michael, and Bob Edwards. 1998b. "Civil Society and Social Capital beyond Putnam," *American Behavioral Scientist* 42 (September): 124–139.

Foot, Philippa. 1977. "Approval and Disapproval," P. M. S. Hacker and J. Raz (eds.), *Law, Morality and Society: Essays in Honour of H. L. A. Hart*. Oxford: Clarendon: 229–246.

Foster, Frances. 1993. "Procedure as a Guarantee of Democracy: The Legacy of the Perestroika Parliament," *Journal of Transnational Law* 25 (April): 1–109.

Foucault, Michel. 1972. *The Archaeology of Knowledge*. New York: Harper and Row.

Foucault, Michel. 1977. *Discipline and Punish: Birth of the Prison*. New York: Pantheon.

Furet, François. 1981. *Interpreting the French Revolution*. Cambridge: Cambridge University Press.

Gaidar, Yegor. 1999. *Days of Defeat and Victory*. Seattle: University of Washington Press.

Ganev, Venelin. 2007. *Preying on the State: The Transformation of Bulgaria after 1989*. Ithaca: Cornell University Press.

Garadzha, Nikita (ed.). 2006. *Suverenitet*. Moscow: Evropa.

Garcelon, Marc. 2005. *Revolutionary Passage: From Soviet to Post-Soviet Russia, 1985–2000*, Philadelphia: Temple University Press.

Geertz, Clifford. 2000. *Local Knowledge: Further Essays in Interpretive Anthropology*. 2nd edn. New York: Basic Books.

Gel'man, Vladimir. 2004. "The Unrule of Law in the Making: The Politics of Informal Institution Building in Russia," *Europe – Asia Studies* 56 (November): 1021–1041.

Gel'man, Vladimir, Sergei Ryzhenkov, and Michael Brie. 2003. *Making and Breaking Democratic Transitions: The Comparative Politics of Russia's Regions*. Lanham, MD: Rowman and Littlefield.

Gilboy, George, and Benjamin Read. 2008. "Political and Social Reform in China: Alive and Walking," *The Washington Quarterly* 31 (Summer): 143–164.

Gleisner, Jeffrey, Leontii Byzov, Nikolai Biryukov, and Victor Sergeyev. 1996. "The Parliament and the Cabinet: Parties, Factions and Parliamentary Control in Russia," *Journal of Contemporary History* 3 (no. 2): 427–461.

Goffman, Erving. 1973. *The Presentation of Self in Everyday Life*. Woodstock, NY: Overlook Press.

Goffman, Erving. 1981. *Forms of Talk*. Philadelphia: University of Pennsylvania Press.

Gorbachev, Mikhail. 1987. *Perestroika: New Thinking for Our Country and the World*. New York: Harper and Row.

Gouldner, Alvin. 1985. *Against Fragmentation*. Oxford: Oxford University Press.

Grace, George. 1987. *The Linguistic Construction of Reality*. London: Croom Helm.

Gramsci, Antonio. 1971. *From the Prison Notebooks*. London: Lawrence and Wishart.

Granovetter, Mark. 1973. "The Strength of Weak Ties," *American Journal of Sociology* 78 (May): 360–380.

Granovetter, Mark. 1982. "The Strength of Weak Ties: A Network Theory Revisited," P. Marsden and N. Lin (eds.), *Social Structure and Network Analysis*. Beverly Hills: Sage: 1005–1030.

Green, David. 1987. *Shaping Political Consciousness*. Ithaca: Cornell University Press.

Greimas, A. J. 1983. *Structural Semantics*. Lincoln: University of Nebraska Press.

Greimas, A. J. 1990a. *The Social Sciences: A Semiotic View*. Minneapolis: University of Minnesota Press.

Greimas, A. J. 1990b. *Narrative Semiotics and Cognitive Discourses*. London: Pinter.

Greskovits, Bela. 1998. *The Political Economy of Protest and Patience: East European and Latin American Transformations Compared*. Budapest: Central European University Press.

Guilhot, Nicolas. 2005. *The Democracy Makers: Human Rights and International Order*. New York: Columbia University Press.

Haas, Ernst. 1991. "Collective Learning: Some Theoretical Speculations," G. Breslauer and P. Tetlock (eds.), *Learning in U.S. and Soviet Foreign Policy*. Boulder, CO: Westview: 62–99.

Habermas, Jürgen. 1970. "On Systematically Distorted Communication," *Inquiry* 13 (Autumn): 205–218.

Habermas, Jürgen. 1971. *Toward a Rational Society*. London: Heinemann.

Habermas, Jürgen. 1974. *Theory and Practice*. London: Heinemann.

Habermas, Jürgen. 1975. *Legitimation Crisis*. Boston: Beacon.

Habermas, Jürgen. 1979. *Communication and the Evolution of Society*. Boston: Beacon.

Habermas, Jürgen. 1984. *The Theory of Communicative Action*. Vol. I: *Reason and the Rationalization of Society*. Boston: Beacon.

Habermas, Jürgen. 1987. *The Theory of Communicative Action*. Vol II: *Lifeworld and System*. Boston: Beacon.

Habermas, Jürgen. 1998. *Between Facts and Norms: Contributions to a Discourse Theory of Law and Democracy*. Cambridge, MA: MIT Press.

Hann, C. M. (ed.). 2002. *Postsocialism: Ideas, Ideologies and Practices in Eurasia*. London: Routledge.

Hart, H. L. A. 1994. *The Concept of Law*. 2nd edn. Oxford: Clarendon.

Havel, Vaclav. 1985. *The Power of the Powerless*. Armonk: M. E. Sharpe.

Hayoz, Nicolas, and Victor Sergeyev. 2003. "Social Networks in Russian Politics," G. Badescu and E. Uslaner (eds.), *Social Capital and the Transition to Democracy*. London: Routledge: 146–160.

Hayri, Aydir, and Gerald McDermott. 1998. "The Network Properties of Corporate Governance and Industrial Restructuring," *Industrial and Corporate Change* 7 (no. 1): 153–194.

Hedlund, Stefan. 1999. *Russia's "Market" Economy: A Bad Case of Predatory Capitalism*. London: UCL Press.

Henderson, Sarah. 2003. *Building Democracy in Contemporary Russia: Western Support for Grassroots Organizations*. Ithaca: Cornell University Press.

Hodge, Robert, and Gunther Kress. 1993. *Language as Ideology*. 2nd edn. London: Routledge.

Holstein, James, and Jaber Gubrium. 2004. "The Active Interview," D. Silverman (ed.), *Qualitative Research: Theory. Method and Practice*. 2nd edn. London: Sage: 140–161.

Horvath, Agnes, and Bjorn Thomassen. 2008. "Mimetic Errors in Liminal Schismogenesis: On the Political Anthropology of the Trickster," *International Political Anthropology* 1 (no. 1): 3–24.

Hosking, Geoffrey. 2004. "Forms of Social Solidarity in Russia and the Soviet Union," I. Markova (ed.), *Trust and Democratic Transition in Post-Communist Europe*. Oxford: Oxford University Press: 47–62.

Howard, Marc. 2003. *The Weakness of Civil Society in Post-Communist Europe*. Cambridge: Cambridge University Press.

Howarth, David *et al*. (eds.). 2000. *Discourse Theory and Political Analysis: Identities, Hegemonies and Social Change*. Manchester: Manchester University Press.

Howarth, David and Yannis Stavrakakis. 2000. "Introducing Discourse Theory and Political Analysis," D. Howarth *et al*. (eds.), *Discourse Theory and Political Analysis: Identities, Hegemonies and Social Change*. Manchester: Manchester University Press: 1–23.

Hughes, James, Peter John, and Gwendolyn Sasse. 2003. "From Plan to Network: Urban Elites and the Postcommunist Organizational State in Russia," *European Journal of Political Research* 41 (no. 3): 395–420.

Humphrey, Caroline. 2004. *The Unmaking of Soviet Life: Everyday Economics after Socialism*. Ithaca: Cornell University Press.

Hunt, Lynn. 1984. *Politics, Culture and Class in the French Revolution*. Berkeley: University of California Press.

Huskey, Eugene. 1990. "Government Rulemaking as a Break on *Perestroika*", *Law and Social Inquiry* 15 (Summer): 419–432.

Huskey, Eugene. 2002. "'Speedy, Just and Fair'? Remaking Legal institutions in Putin's Russia." Unpublished manuscript, Stetson University, DeLand, FL.

Huskey, Eugene. 2004. "From Higher Party Schools to Academies of State Service: The Marketization of Bureaucratic Training in Russia," *Slavic Review* 63 (Summer): 325–348.

Huskey, Eugene. 2005. "Putin as Patron: Cadres Policy in the Russian Transition," A. Pravda (ed.), *Leading Russia: Putin in Perspective. Essays in Honour of Archie Brown*. Oxford: Oxford University Press: 1–28.

Huskey, Eugene. 2007. "The Politics-Administration Nexus in Postcommunist Russia." Paper presented at the Annual Meeting of the American Association for the Advancement of Slavic Studies, New Orleans, Louisiana (November 15–18, 2007).

Itar-Tass. 2008. "President Medvedev Acknowledges Deficit of High-rank Officials in Russia," July 24 (in Johnson's Russia List, July 25, 2008).

Jameson, Fredric. 1981. *The Political Unconscious*. Ithaca: Cornell University Press.

Jameson, Fredric. 1998. *The Cultural Turn: Selected Writings on the Postmodern, 1983–1998*. London: Verso.

Jowitt, Kenneth. 1992. *New World Disorder: The Leninist Extinction*. Berkeley: University of California Press.

Keenan, Edward. 1986. "Muscovite Political Folkways," *Russian Review* 45 (no. 2): 115–181.

Kharkhordin, Oleg. 1998. "Civil Society and Orthodox Christianity," *Europe–Asia Studies* 50 (September): 949–968.

Kharkhordin, Oleg. 2000. *The Collective and the Individual in Russia: A Study of Practices*. Berkeley: University of California Press.

Kharkhordin, Oleg. 2009a. "Druzhba: klassicheskaya teoriya i sovremennye zaboty," O. Kharkhordin (ed.), *Druzhba: ocherki po teorii praktik*. St. Petersburg: European University at St. Petersburg: 11–47.

Kharkhordin, Oleg. 2009b. "Posleslovie. Druzhba: pere-sbora?" O. Kharkhordin (ed.), *Druzhba: ocherki po teorii praktik*. Saint Petersburg: European University at Saint Petersburg: 424–455.

Kolankiewicz, George. 1992. "The Reconstruction of Citizenship: Reverse Incorporation in Eastern Europe," K. Poznanski (ed.), *Constructing Capitalism: The Reemergence of Civil Society and the Liberal Economy in the Post-Communist World*. Boulder, CO: Westview: 141–158.

Kollmann, Nancy. 1987. *Kinship and Politics: The Making of the Muscovite Political System 1345–1547*. Stanford: Stanford University Press.

Kollmann, Nancy. 1999. *By Honor Bound: State and Society in Early Modern Russia*. Ithaca: Cornell University Press.

Kryshtanovskaya, Olga. 2005. Interviewed by E. Korop, *Profil*, no. 10, March 21 (in Johnson's Russia List, Mar. 28, 2005).

Kryshtanovskaya, Olga and Stephen White. 2005. "Inside the Putin Court: A Research Note," *Europe–Asia Studies* 57 (November): 1065–1075.

Kubik, Jan. 2003. "Cultural Legacies of State Socialism: History Making and Cultural-Political Entrepreneurship in Postcommunist Poland and Russia," G. Ekiert and S. Hanson (eds.), *Capitalism and Democracy in Central and Eastern Europe: Assessing the Legacy of Communist Rule*. Cambridge: Cambridge University Press: 317–351.

Kubik, Jan. 2005. "How to Study Civil Society: The State of the Art and What to Do Next," *East European Politics and Society* 19 (no. 1): 105–120.

Kurkchiyan, Marina. 2003. "The Illegitimacy of Law in Post-Soviet Societies," D. Galligan and M. Kurkchiyan (eds.), *Law and Informal Practices*. Oxford: Oxford University Press: 25–46.

Laclau, Ernesto. 2005. *On Populist Reason*. London: Verso.

Laclau, Ernesto and Chantal Mouffe. 2001. *Hegemony and Socialist Strategy: Towards a Radical Democratic Politics*. 2nd edn. London: Verso.

Lakoff, George. 1996. *Moral Politics: What Conservatives Know That Liberals Don't*. Chicago: University of Chicago Press.

Lakoff, George. 2008. *The Political Mind: Why You Can't Understand 21st-Century Politics with an 18th-Century Brain*. New York. Viking.

Lapidus, Gail. 1991. "State and Society: Toward the Emergence of Civil Society in the Soviet Union," A. Dallin and G. Lapidus (eds.), *The Soviet System in Crisis*. Boulder, CO: Westview: 130–150.

Lazar, Annita, and Michelle Lazar. 2004. "The Discourse of the New World Order: Out-Casting the Double Face of Threat," *Discourse & Society* 15 (nos. 2–3): 223–242.

Ledeneva, Alena. 1998. *Russia's Informal Economy of Favours*. Cambridge: Cambridge University Press.

Ledeneva, Alena. 2004a. "Underground Financing in Russia," J. Kornai, B. Rothstein and S. Rose-Ackerman (eds.), *Creating Social Trust in Post-Communist Transition*. New York: Palgrave Macmillan: 71–90.

Ledeneva, Alena. 2004b. "The Geneology of Krugovaya Poruka: Forced Trust as a Feature of Russian Political Culture," I. Markova (ed.), *Trust and Democratic Transition in Post-Communist Europe*. Oxford: Oxford University Press: 85–108.

Ledeneva, Alena. 2006. *How Russia Really Works: The Informal Practices That Shaped Post-Soviet Politics and Business*. Ithaca: Cornell University Press.

Lefebrve, Henri. 1969. *The Sociology of Marx*. New York: Vintage Books.

Lemon, Alaina. 2000. *Between Two Fires: Gypsy Performance and Romani Memory from Pushkin to Post-Socialism*. Durham, NC: Duke University Press.

Lenin, V. I. [1902] 1969. *What Is to Be Done?* New Work: International Publishers.

Leont'ev, Mikhail. 1991a. "My khotim obmanut istoriyu," *Nezavisimaya gazeta*, October 22.

Leont'ev, Mikhail. 1991b. "Novoe pravitel'stvo Rossii," *Nezavisimaya gazeta*, November 9 November.

Lomax, Bill. 1997. "The Strange Death of 'Civil Society' in Post-Communist Hungary," *Journal of Communist Studies and Transition Politics* 13 (March): 41–63.

Lotman, Yuri. 1990. *Universe of the Mind: A Semiotic Theory of Culture*. Bloomington: Indiana University Press.

Lotman, Yuri. 1992. *Kul'tura i vzryv*. Moscow: Gnozis.

Lukacs, George. [1919] 1971. *History and Class Consciousness*. Cambridge, MA: MIT Press.

Lundh, Patrik. 2008. "Cultivating Rights: Russia's Rights Defenders and the Interstices of Formal and Informal Morality." Doctoral dissertation, University of California, Santa Cruz, CA.

Lvov, Georgii. 1991. "Plan rossiiskoi reformy pochti gotov," *Nezavisimaya gazeta*, October 22.

MacFarlane, S. Neil. 2003. "Politics and the Rule of Law in the Commonwealth of Independent States," D. Galligan and M. Kurkchiyan (eds.). *Law and Informal Practices: The Post-Communist Experience*. Oxford: Oxford University Press: 61–76.

Makarkin, Aleksei. 2004. "Za vlast' v sovetakh direktorov," *Ezhenedelnyi zhurnal*. October 3: 20–23.

Marsh, Christopher. 2000. "Civic Community, Communist Support, and Democratization in Russia: The View from Smolensk," *Demokratizatsiya* 8 (Fall): 447–460.

Marx, Karl. [1867] 1906. *Capital*. Vol. I. Chicago: Charles Kerr.

Marx, Karl. and Frederick Engels. [1932] 1965. *The German Ideology*. London: Lawrence and Wishart.

Mbeke, Achille. 2001. *On the Postcolony*. Berkeley: University of California Press.

Michnik, Adam. 1985. *Letters from Prison and Other Essays*. Berkeley: University of California Press.

Mihaylova, Dimitrina. 2004. *Social Capital in Central and Eastern Europe: A Critical Assessment and Literature Review*. Budapest: Central European University.

Mitchell, Timothy. 1999. "Society, Economy and the State Effect," G. Steinmetz (ed.), *State/Culture: State Formation after the Cultural Turn*. Ithaca: Cornell University Press: 76–97.

Miller, Jody, and Barry Glassner. 2004. The 'Inside' and the 'Outside': Finding Realities in Interviews," D. Silverman (ed.), *Qualitative Research: Theory, Method and Practice*. London: Sage: 125–139.

Mische, Ann. 2003. "Cross-Talk in Movements: Reconceiving the Culture-Network Link," M. Diani and D. McAdam (eds.), *Social Movements and Networks: Relational Approaches to Collective Action*. Oxford: Oxford University Press: 258–280.

Myant, Martin. 2005. "Klaus, Havel and the Debate over Civil Society in the Czech Republic," *Journal of Communist Studies and Transition Politics* 21 (June): 248–267.

Newton, Kenneth. 1997. "Social Capital and Democracy," *American Behavioral Scientist* 40 (March/April): 575–586.

Pavlovskii, Gleb (ed.). 2007. *PRO suverennuyu demokratiyu*. Moscow: Evropa.

Pesmen, Dale. 2000. *Russia and Soul: An Exploration*. Ithaca: Cornell University Press.

Polyakov, Leonid. 2007. "Predislovie," G. Pavlovskii (ed.), *PRO suverennuyu demokratiyu*. Moscow: Evropa.

Pribylovskii, Vladimir. 2005. "Proiskhozhdenie putinskoi oligarkii. Prezidentskoe okruzhenie: dos'e, svyazi, vozmozhnie naznacheniya. Chast' 1," www.polit.ru, October 19: 1–16.

Przeworski, Adam. 1991. *Democracy and the Market: Political and Economic Reforms in Eastern Europe and Latin America*. Cambridge: Cambridge University Press.

Putnam, Robert. 1993. *Making Democracy Work: Civic Traditions in Modern Italy*. Princeton: Princeton University Press.

Putnam, Robert. 2001. *Bowling Alone: The Collapse and Revival of American Community*. New York: Touchstone.

Quigley, Kevin. 2000. "Lofty Goals, Modest Results: Assisting Civil Society in Eastern Europe," M. Ottaway and T. Carothers (eds.), *Funding Virtue: Civil Society Aid and Democracy Promotion*. Washington, DC: Carnegie Endowment for International Peace: 191–215.

Radaev, Vadim. 2004. "How Trust Is Established in Economic Relationships When Institutions and Individuals Are Not Trustworthy: The Case of Russia," J. Kornai, B. Rothstein and S. Rose-Ackerman (eds.), *Creating Social Trust in Post-Socialist Transition*. New York: Palgrave Macmillan: 91–110.

Read, Benjamin. 2008. "Assessing Variations in Civil Society Organizations: China's Homeowner Associations in Comparative Perspective," *Comparative Political Studies* 41 (September): 1240–1265.

Reddaway, Peter, and Dmitri Glinski. 2001. *The Tragedy of Russia's Reforms: Market Bolshevism against Democracy*. Washington, DC: US Institute of Peace.

Rigby, T. H., and Bohdan Harasymiw (eds.). 1983. *Leadership Selection and Patron–Client Relations in the USSR and Yugoslavia*. London: George Allen and Unwin.

Ries, Nancy. 1997. *Russian Talk: Culture and Conversation during Perestroika*. Ithaca: Cornell University Press.

Rodriguez, Dylan. 2007. "The Political Logic of the Non-Profit Industrial Complex," Incite! Women of Color against Violence (ed.), *The Revolution Will Not Be Funded: Beyond the Non-Profit Industrial Complex*. Cambridge. MA: South End Press: 21–40.

Rogozhnikov, Mikhail. 2007. "Chto takoe 'suverennaya demokratiya'," G. Pavlovskii (ed.), *PRO suverennuyu demokratiyu*. Moscow: Evropa: 27–32.

Rothstein, Bo. 2004. "Social Trust and Honesty in Government: A Causal Mechanisms Approach," J. Kornai, B. Rothstein and S. Rose-Ackerman (eds.), *Creating Social Trust in Post-Socialist Transition*. New York: Palgrave Macmillan: 13–30.

Roy, Oliver. 2000. *The New Central Asia: The Creation of Nations*. New York: New York University Press.

Sakwa, Richard. 2006. "From Revolution to *Krizis*: The Transcending Revolutions of 1989–91," *Comparative Politics* 38 (July): 459–478.

Salin, Pavel. 2007. "Mnogopolyusnaya politcheskaya Rossiya," *Politicheskii klass,* no. 32 (July 18). www.politklass.ru/cgi-bin/issue.pl?id=854.

Samarina, Alexandra. 2008. "President Outraged by the Duma's Stance," *Nezavisimaya gazeta,* December 17 (trans. and publ. in Johnson's Russia List, December 17, 2008).

Saussure, Ferdinand de. [1972] 1983. *Course in General Linguistics.* LaSalle, IL: Open Court.

Schatz, Edward. 2004. *Modern Clan Politics: The Power of Blood in Kazakhstan and Beyond.* Seattle: University of Washington Press.

Schmidt-Pfister, Diana. 2008. "What Kind of Civil Society in Russia?" S. White (ed.), *Culture and Society in Putin's Russia.* Basingstoke: Palgrave Macmillan: 37–71.

Schoenman, Roger. 2002. "Parties for Profit: The Impacts of Networks on State-Building in Poland, Romania and Bulgaria." Paper presented at the Annual Meeting of the American Association for the Advancement of Slavic Studies, Pittsburgh, PA.

Schumpeter, Joseph. 1962. *Capitalism, Socialism and Democracy.* New York: Harper and Row.

Scott, James. 1998. *Seeing Like a State: How Certain Schemes to Improve the Human Condition Have Failed.* New Haven: Yale University Press.

Seidman, Harold. 1975. *Politics, Position and Power: The Dynamics of Federal Organization. New York:* Oxford: Oxford University Press.

Seligman, Alan. 2002. "Civil Society as Idea and Ideal," S. Chambers and W. Kymlicka (eds.), *Alternative Conceptions of Civil Society.* Princeton: Princeton University Press: 13–33.

Sergeyev, Victor, and Nikolai Biryukov. 1993. *Russia's Road to Democracy: Parliament, Communism and Traditional Culture.* Aldershot, UK: Edward Elgar.

Sergeyev, Victor, and Nikolai Biryukov. 1997. *Russia's Politics in Transition.* Aldershot, UK: Ashgate.

Sewell, Willliam, Jr. 1994. *A Rhetoric of Bourgeois Revolution: The Abbé Sieyes and What Is the Third Estate.* Durham, NC: Duke University Press.

Sewell, Willliam, Jr. 1999. "The Concept(s) of Culture," V. Bonnell and L. Hunt (eds.), *Beyond the Cultural Turn.* Berkeley: University of California Press: 35–61.

Shevchenko, Olga. 2008. *Crisis and the Everyday in Postsocialist Moscow.* Bloomington: Indiana University Press.

Smith, Kathleen. 2002. *Mythmaking in the New Russia: Politics and Memory during the Yeltsin Era.* Ithaca: Cornell University Press.

Solnick, Steven. 1998. *Stealing the State: Control and Collapse in Soviet Institutions.* Cambridge, MA: Harvard University Press.

Solomon, Peter. 1987. "The Case of the Vanishing Acquittal: Informal Norms and the Practice of Soviet Criminal Justice," *Soviet Studies* 39 (October): 531–555.

Solomon, Peter. 2007. "Informal Practices in Russian Justice: Probing the Limits of Post-Soviet Reform," F. Feldbrugge (ed.). *Russia, Europe and the Rule of Law.* Leiden: Martinus Nijhoff: 79–91.

Solomon, Peter. 2008. "Law in Public Administration: How Russia Differs," *Journal of Communist Studies and Transition Politics* 24 (March): 115–135.

Stark, David. 1997. "Recombinant Property in East European Capitalism," G. Grabher and D. Stark (eds.), *Restructuring Networks in Post-Socialism.* Oxford: Oxford University Press: 35–69.

Stark, David and Laslo Bruszt. 1998. *Postsocialist Pathways: Transforming Politics and Property in East Central Europe.* Cambridge: Cambridge University Press.

Stark, David and Vedres Balasz. 2006. "Social Times of Network Spaces: Network Sequence Analysis of Network Formation and Foreign Investment in Hungary, 1987–2001," *American Journal of Sociology* 3 (March): 1367–1411.

Starr, S. Frederick. 1989. "Soviet Union: A Civil Society," *Foreign Policy* 70 (Spring): 26–41.

Sundstrom, Lisa. 2006. *Funding Civil Society: Foreign Assistance and NGO Development in Russia.* Stanford: Stanford University Press.

Surkov, Vladislav. 2007. "Suverenitet – eto politicheskii sinonim konkurentospo-sobnosti," G. Pavlovskii (ed.). *PRO suverennuyu demokratiyu.* Moscow: Evropa: 33–61.

Swartz, David. 2003. "Pierre Bourdieu's Political Sociology and Governance Perspective," H. Bang (ed.), *Governance as Social and Political Communication.* Manchester: Manchester University Press: 140–158.

Tarrow, Sidney. 1996. "Making Social Science Work across Space and Time: A Critical Reflection on Robert Putnam's *Making Democracy Work,*" *American Political Science Review* 90 (June): 389–397.

Tilly, Charles. 1999. "Epilogue: Now Where?" G. Steinmetz (ed.) *State/Culture: State Formation and the Cultural Turn.* Ithaca: Cornell University Press: 407–419.

Torfing, Jacob. 1999. *New Theories of Discourse: Laclau, Mouffe and Zizek.* Oxford: Blackwell.

Urban, Michael. 1985. "Conceptualizing Political Power in the USSR: Patterns of Binding and Bonding," *Studies in Comparative Communism* 18 (Winter): 207–226.

Urban, Michael. 1989. *An Algebra of Soviet Power: Elite Circulation in the Belorussian Republic 1966–1986.* Cambridge: Cambridge University Press.

Urban, Michael. 1990. *More Power to the Soviets: The Democratic Revolution in the USSR.* Aldershot, UK: Edward Elgar.

Urban, Michael. 1994a. "December 1993 as a Replication of Late-Soviet Electoral Practices," *Post-Soviet Affairs* 10 (April–June): 127–158.

Urban, Michael. 1994b. "The Politics of Identity in Russia's Postcommunist Transition: The Nation against Itself," *Slavic Review* 53 (Fall): 733–765.

Urban, Michael. 1996. "Stages of Political Identity Formation in Late Soviet and Post-Soviet Russia," V. Bonnell (ed.), *Identities in Transition: Eastern Europe and Russia after the Collapse of Communism*. Berkeley: International and Area Studies, University of California: 140–154.

Urban, Michael. 1997. *The Rebirth of Politics in Russia*. Cambridge: Cambridge University Press.

Urban, Michael. 1998. "Remythologizing the Russian State," *Europe–Asia Studies* 50 (September): 969–992.

Urban, Michael. 2003. "Social Relations and Political Practices in Post-Communist Russia," D. Kelley (ed.), *After Communism: Perspectives on Democracy*. Fayetteville: University of Arkansas Press: 119–142.

Urban, Michael. 2004. *Russia Gets the Blues: Music, Culture and Community in Unsettled Times*. Ithaca: Cornell University Press.

Urban, Michael. 2006. "Post-Soviet Political Discourse and the Creation of Political Communities," A. Schönle (ed.), *Lotman and Cultural Studies: Encounters and Extensions*. Madison: University of Wisconsin Press: 115–135.

Van Dijk, Teun. 2003. "The Discourse–Knowledge Interface," G. Weiss and R. Wodak (eds.), *Critical Discourse Analysis: Theory and Interdisciplinarity*. New York: Palgrave Macmillan: 85–109.

Van Dijk, Teun. 2006. "Discourse and Manipulation," *Discourse & Society* 17 (no. 3): 359–383.

Verdery, Katherine. 1996. *What Was Socialism and What Comes Next?* Princeton: Princeton University Press.

Verdery, Katherine. 2003. *The Vanishing Hectare: Property and Value in Postsocialist Transylvania*. Ithaca: Cornell University Press.

Volkov, Vadim. 2002. *Violent Entrepreneurs*. Ithaca: Cornell University Press.

Volkov, Vadim. 2004. "The Selective Use of State Capacity in Russia's Economy: Property Disputes and Enterprise Takeovers, 1998–2002." J. Kornai, B. Rothsetin and S. Rose-Ackerman (eds.), *Creating Social Trust in Post-Socialist Transition*. New York: Palgrave Macmillan: 126–147.

Volkov, Vadim. 2008. "Russia's New 'State Corporations': Locomotives of Modernization or Covert Privatization Schemes?" *Policy Memo, Program on New Approaches to Russian Security*. St. Petersburg: European University at St. Petersburg.

Walzer, Michael. 2002. "Equality and Civil Society," S. Chambers and W. Kymlicka (eds.), *Alternative Conceptions of Civil Society*. Princeton: Princeton University Press: 34–49.

Weber, Max. [1919] 1946. "Politics as a Vocation," H. H. Gerth and C. W. Mills (eds.), *From Max Weber: Essays in Sociology*. New York: Oxford University Press: 77–128.

Weber, Max. 1947. *The Theory of Social and Economic Organizations* New York: The Free Press.

Wedeen, Lisa. 2008. *Peripheral Visions: Publics, Power and Performance*. Chicago: University of Chicago Press.

Wedel, Janine. 1998. *Collision and Collusion: The Strange Case of Western Aid to Eastern Europe*. New York: St. Martin's Press.

Wedel, Janine. 2005. "Flex Organizing and the Clan-State," W. Pridemore (ed.), *Ruling Russia: Law, Crime and Justice in a Changing Society*. Lanham, MD: Rowman and Littlefield: 101–116.

White, David. 2006. *The Russian Democratic Party Yabloko: Opposition in a Managed Democracy*. Aldershot, UK: Ashgate.

White, Harrison. 1992. *Identity and Control: A Structural Theory of Social Action*. Princeton: Princeton University Press.

White, Stephen. 2005. "Political Disengagement in Post-Communist Russia: A Qualitative Study," *Europe–Asia Studies* 57 (December): 1121–1142.

White, Stephen and Ian McAllister. 2008. "The Putin Phenomenon," *Journal of Communist Studies and Transition Politics* 24 (December): 604–628.

Wiegle, Marcia, and Jim Butterfield. 1992. "Civil Society in Reforming Communist Regimes: the Logic of Emergence," *Comparative Politics* 25 (October): 1–23.

Williams, Glyn. 1999. *French Discourse Analysis: The Method of Post-Structuralism*. London: Routledge.

Willerton, John. 1992. *Patronage and Politics in the USSR*. Cambridge: Cambridge University Press.

Yavlinskii, G. A. *et al.* 1995. *Reformy dlya bol'shinstva*. Moscow: Ob"edinenie Yabloko.

Zarycki, Tomasz. 2003. "Cultural Capital and the Political Role of the Intelligentsia in Poland," *Journal of Communist Studies and Transition Politics* 19 (December): 91–108.

Zylko, Boguslaw. 2001. "Culture and Semiotics: Notes on Lotman's Conception of Culture," *New Literary History* 32: 391–408.

Index